W9-BRP-586

"THE MAN WHO COULD DO NO WRONG"

"THE MAN WHO COULD DO NO WRONG"

CHARLES BLAIR

with

John and Elizabeth Sherrill

Published by

Lincoln, Virginia 22078

Library of Congress Cataloging in Publication Data

Blair, Charles E.
The man who could do no wrong.

1. Blair, Charles E. 2. Calvary Temple (Denver, Colo.)—Biography 3. Clergy—Colorado—Biography. 4. Denver (Colo.)—Biography. I. Sherrill, John L. II. Sherrill, Elizabeth. III. Title.
BX9999.D463B54 289 [B] 81-10072
ISBN 0-912376-71-6 AACR2

The Man Who Could Do No Wrong

Published by
Chosen Books Publishing Company, Ltd.,
Lincoln, Virginia 22078

Dedication

To my family . . .

who provided me with a haven where I could come in out of the storm . . .

especially my wife Betty whose constancy strengthened me in the Lord . . .

and my daughters Vicki and Judy and their families who were always there when I needed them.

To my staff . . .

who "hung in there" when the going was rough . . .

especially Joan Bjork my devoted secretary of 25 years who served without counting the cost.

To my friends and colleagues . . .

who would not let me carry this burden alone.

They came from far away to pray, to listen, to be near . . .

especially Gene Martin, my beloved friend since seminary days . . .

and Harvey Rhodig, a stalwart companion for over 33 years.

To my extended family, the congregation of Calvary Temple . . .

who in the face of crisis and adverse publicity were quick to move and slow to judge.

Above all, to my blessed Lord . . .

Who spoke to me through them all. Through the Word, through circumstances, through family and friends and through His body He assured me that my failure had not destroyed His all-sufficient love.

Writers' Foreword:

The Christian's Secret of Handling a Mistake

It was one of those moments when our own fallibility was painfully apparent. We'd made a mistake. Not the biggest one we'd ever made, and doubtless not the last. But a mistake nonetheless, and it left us smarting. That was our mood when the phone call came from our friend the "Galloping Gourmet," Graham Kerr.

"Treena and I are in Denver," Graham said. "We'd like you to pray for some friends of ours."

The friends, from whose home Graham was calling, were a pastor and his wife. Not just any pastor, either. Charles E. Blair, Graham told us, had the largest church in Denver and one of the biggest in the country, a huge TV and radio ministry, missionary outreach all over the world.

And this Christian leader had just been hauled into court on a charge of fraud.

The case, apparently, stemmed from an illegal sale of securities. Since Charles was so well known the papers were playing it to the hilt. "We don't know the legal rights and wrongs," Graham said. "It's Charles and Betty themselves we're concerned about."

"How are they handling the emotions of it?" we asked, with more than abstract curiosity.

"That's where your prayers come in. They're going through agony." Every instinct, he said, was telling Charles to run away and hide. "But he knows with his mind that *God has a better answer to mistakes.* Will you pray with us that he'll hang in there till he finds it?"

Not only would we pray; we knew right then that these were people we wanted to meet. In the years since, we've made many trips to Denver. We've stayed in Charles' and Betty's home, we've traveled together, we've laughed together and we've cried together.

We've come to know them intimately, from Charles' Depression-blighted childhood . . . to success beyond his wildest dreams . . . to public humiliation. Charles came to stand in our minds for every one of us caught in the trap of his own image. Needing to appear successful, wise, happy—allowing ourselves no room for failure.

His story could be all our stories, only written in capital letters. For few of us have started with so little, achieved so much, lost so publicly. What he learned in the process is so very practical, has helped us so much in handling our own mistakes, that we want to share it with all the other error-prone people in search of the Christian's secret.

John and Elizabeth Sherrill
Chappaqua, New York

I had not yet seen the morning paper.

I hummed as I looked through the rows of ties in my closet. Selecting a grey one with a broad yellow stripe I turned my attention to the shoe rack. A minister could never be too careful of his appearance.

A starched white handkerchief barely protruding from my suit jacket and I was ready to head for my office at church. There was nothing special on the agenda today—just the usual round of committee meetings with hopefully enough time to dictate a sermon outline to my secretary. It was just that I took very seriously the matter of a minister's image. Not just his clothes, of course. His family life, his hobbies, the books he read, all had to be above reproach.

Even his car, I thought, as I swung my conservative grey "98" Olds into the huge church parking lot. Even at this early hour, eight o'clock on a Thursday morning, there were perhaps 75 cars already at the church. Some belonged to members of our 24-hour prayer team, some to men attending a prayer breakfast, others to custodians cleaning up after the previous evening's events. Ten thousand people a week passed through these doors.

I let myself in the side door nearest my study, then on an impulse turned left, walked down a corridor and pushed open the door to the sanctuary. I stood for a long moment in the immense fan-shaped room, the March sunlight streaming through the tall stained-glass panels in the east wall, throwing splashes of color on the walnut pews.

I often stepped in here in the morning, before my office staff assembled, to marvel anew in the quiet at what God had done. That He had used *me,* that was the wonder I could never get over. Me, the kid from the wrong side of the tracks, the least likely person on earth to build anything like this. The huge room seated 2,300 people, but for each of the three Sunday services we had to set up extra chairs along the walls. Three months ago the church board had voted to erect a new sanctuary more than twice this size on land we owned just to the north; at 10:00 a.m. I was due at a nearby coffee shop to discuss preliminary plans with an architect.

My secretary, Joan Bjork, was already at her desk when I stepped into my office. I had an 8:30 conference, she reminded me, with the producer of my daily radio show. That was barely concluded when the director of one of the church's eight choirs arrived to discuss the Easter music. A phone conversation with a company installing new TV cameras in the sanctuary lasted longer than I expected, and when Joan was able to buzz me I was ten minutes overdue for my appointment with the architect.

Fortunately the Cherry Creek motel was only a five-minute drive away, and I found a parking place right at the entrance. I walked quickly through the lobby and scanned the booths in the coffee shop: good, the other man was late too. "Morning, Maggie," I said. "No one's been in asking for me?"

The white-haired hostess, a longtime acquaintance, appeared to be having some kind of difficulty with a pile of receipts in front of her.

"No," she said without looking up.

Usually Maggie asked after my wife or our daughters or one of our grandchildren, but I waited a moment and she said no more. Didn't give me a menu either—well, all I ever ordered at this time of day was coffee.

I chose a booth where I could watch the lobby. The waitress was another old friend. But she too seemed preoccupied as she took out her pad, offering no comment on last night's hockey game.

"Just the usual," I told her.

"Coffee?" she asked in a voice so distant that I looked up in surprise.

"Yes, please. Coffee."

"And what did you want in it?"

"Why, same as always." When she still maintained a noncommital stare: "Black—you know."

It seemed to me the coffee was a long time coming. A man sat down in the booth across from me and opened a copy of the *Rocky Mountain News*. And still the architect had not appeared. At last the waitress set the coffee in front of me, then swiftly returned to the kitchen. I lifted the cup to my lips.

And there I froze.

Staring at me from the front page of the *News* across the way was my own picture.

Coffee splashed into the saucer as I set down the cup. With me in the photograph was an attorney and the Denver district judge with whom we had met the day before. I remembered a newspaper photographer at the hearing—but nothing had transpired that was front page news!

I stood up, fumbled in my pocket and dropped a bill on the table. On the registration desk in the lobby was a pile of newspapers. I snatched up the top one, flung a quarter on the pile and escaped through the glass double doors.

In the car I scanned the picture caption:

Blair and Attorney Listen at Hearing.

Then in smaller type: *The Reverend Charles E. Blair, left, and his attorney, listened during a hearing conducted Wednesday by Chief Denver Dist. Judge Robert T. Kingsley, right, on a State Securities Division complaint that Blair and three corporations he created have defrauded investors.*

At the word *defrauded* the newsprint seemed to spin before my eyes. Why had I parked in this conspicuous spot right at the door! I started the motor and drove a block from the motel. On a side street I pulled over and turned, as the caption directed, to page five.

And there the world of my carefully cultivated image came to an end. The headline looked three feet fall:

REVEREND CHARLES E. BLAIR ACCUSED OF INVESTOR FRAUD

Popular Denver minister, the Reverend Charles E. Blair and three nonprofit corporations he created were accused by the state Wednesday of defrauding investors. . . .

Calvary Temple, a wedge-shaped building at 200 S. University Boulevard, houses Denver's largest congregation and is among the ten largest churches in the nation. . . .

It was a long article, running onto a second inside page. Most of it was of a technical nature, having to do with the place and nature of the hearing, the distinction between "Time Payment Certificates" and "Call Payment Certificates" and other terms I scarcely understood myself. Portions of it, however, were only too clear:

The three corporations have raised a total of about 14 million dollars from about 3,400 investors through the sale of securities and bonds. . . . Assistant Attorney General Andrew Markus told Kingsley that most of the investors are elderly and some invested their life savings. . . .

The article pointed out that no investor had, in fact, actually lost money, but the *impression* left was one of dishonest dealing. The headline over the conclusion of the story hammered home the theme again:

BLAIR, THREE CORPORATIONS
ACCUSED OF DEFRAUDING INVESTORS

The big black letters blurred before my eyes. I squeezed them shut trying to recall the meeting in that judge's office yesterday. There were so many meetings, so many activities the church was involved in. This had been just one of the many sessions involving the sale of bonds, in one of our frequent expansion drives.

For months—years now—we'd been in touch with the Securities and Exchange Commission trying to get approval on a prospectus to complete our geriatric center and nursing home. With the tight money of the past few years, progress on this, as on other church projects, had been slower than anticipated, but those who had invested their money would get every penny back. We had financial people working on a plan to protect them right now; I had gone yesterday to outline it before a district judge.

I also knew that intentions were not the point. Early in life I had learned that *the point was what people thought*. The image you presented. In this article, with the linking over and over of my name and the word *fraud*—the image was of a cheat and a liar. CHARLES BLAIR ACCUSED OF FRAUD.

How could I stand in the pulpit next Sunday? How could I even walk down a street? My face went into a million-and-a-half living rooms every Sunday morning. I pictured this paper arriving at each of these homes.

I wished I were invisible. A couple was walking toward me down the sidewalk. I slid lower in the seat. Don't let it be anyone I know! They passed and I breathed again.

And suddenly I was seeing myself peering through another window, scanning another street, hoping against hope there was no one who knew me. . . .

2

It was during the Depression in Enid, Oklahoma, and the window was the only one in the tiny front room which served our family as living room, kitchen, dining room, weekly bath room and, at night, my sister's bedroom. It was one of the smallest houses in Enid, part of a row of old frame cottages. But the special drawback to me, at age 11, was that it was directly across the street from my school, so that there was no hiding from the other kids the kind of house we lived in.

The worst part of the day came now when I had to step out of the door carrying the metal pail that told the world the Blairs got charity milk from the government. That was why I hung about the window after school, watching the playground across the street, waiting for the last straggler to head for home.

"Charles! Haven't you gone yet?" Mother came indoors with a basket of wash from the clothesline. "If you don't hurry there'll be none left!"

I picked up the hated pail, but out on the porch I set it down again. Duke Everett was practicing figure-8's on his bicycle in the teachers' parking lot. At last he pedalled off. I glanced right and left along the street, grabbed the pail and started out at a run. The surplus milk was passed out at an old firehouse four blocks away. The officials sat in the wide doorway while we lined up with our pails on the sidewalk, exposed to the stares of passersby.

The line inched forward; I handed in our pail to be filled. Then I replaced the metal lid and started home. This part of the trip took longer, the heavy pail bumping against my leg, the thin wire handle cutting a ridge in the flesh of my palm. At the corner of our street I saw my father turning in to our house. I could tell by the sag in his muscular shoulders that once more he had found no work.

I had almost caught up with him, was almost safe inside, when Duke Everett appeared at the end of the street. With my whole soul I coveted a bike of any kind, but especially a sleek red beauty like his with black rubber hand grips and a diamond-shaped reflector. He sped like a young god down the street and came to a daring standing stop right at our front step.

"Whachya got in the pail, Charlie?" he jeered.

"Whiskey!" I shouted back, though I knew Dad would tan the hide off me if he overheard.

"My mom buys our milk at the store," Duke pressed his advantage, but I crossed our porch at a bound and slammed the front door behind me.

"About time!" my mother said, extricating herself from my father's embrace and taking the pail from me. She carried it to the corner we called the kitchen, where on the single gas burner the perpetual pot of cornmeal mush was simmering. Mush for breakfast, mush for dinner, mush for supper—without the government milk we would have gone hungry indeed.

Dad pulled a pouch of Bull Durham tobacco from his pocket and rolled a cigarette, as he did each day on reaching home. But I stayed rooted inside the door. Duke's scornful laugh, the glint of the afternoon sun on his handlebars, had struck something unsuspected deep inside me. "No one, ever," this unfamiliar self proclaimed, "is going to look down on me again. . . ."

Before we went on the milk dole, our poverty had had no shame to it. My father may not have made much money, but his work was exacting and respected. He was a lineman with the electric company, the man whose job it was to climb the tall poles and string the high-voltage electric wires between them.

All during the 1920s, each time a new power station was built in Texas, Kansas, Oklahoma, the call would go out for these skilled men and we would pile our belongings into our old car and go to where the row of newly erected poles stretched to infinity across the prairie. For weeks and months Dad would be part of a team who dragged the lines aloft, fastened them to the crossbars, and looped them to the next bar in a precise dipping arch, bringing electricity to areas where it had never come before.

Then the job would be completed and we would move again, to another rented house, enroll in another school. This part was hard on my sister Bertha Mae, four years older than I, because she took school seriously. I never minded dropping classwork, at which I was generally behind; my problems were on the playground. My dad was a big tall man with muscles hard as one of his own poles, but I took after Mother, small-boned and fragile-looking, and at each new school I had to prove myself with my fists.

My brother Bob, four years younger and the baby of the family, had no such problems. During most of these wandering years he was too young to be in school and when he did start he had my reputation as a fighter to protect him.

Linemen were paid well enough when they worked; the problem was that months would pass when no new electrification was going in, and that was when we tightened our belts. We were a sober, close-knit family, strangers in any community where we happened to be, drawing our strength from one another. In the late afternoons we kids would work the butter churn while Mother cut down an elbowless shirt of

Dad's to fit Bob or me. I never saw my mother sit down without a pile of sewing in her lap.

When Dad was working, his return home was the high point of any day. We knew he was back when we would hear his lineman's belt and hooks thump onto the floor of the porch. The heavy belt was long enough to pass around both his waist and the pole, but it was the hooks I liked: steel leg rods ending in eight-inch spikes designed for digging into the sides of the pole as he climbed.

The hooks would clatter to the floor and Dad would roar into the house, shouting Mother's name, filling the air with noise and energy. He was a large, rough-mannered man and Mother was the center of his world. I don't think he knew he was shouting, it was simply the only tone of voice he had. He would burst into the kitchen, black from the sticky creosote which covered the poles, and take her in his arms, leaving creosote handprints among the printed flowers on her dress.

If we were poor we were no worse off than many families in small prairie towns in the 1920s. Wherever we moved Mother would start a vegetable garden out back and raise a few chickens, so that there was always enough to eat, and even occasionally some extra pennies that Bertha Mae and Bob and I could take to the store for bubble gum.

The only shadow on our lives in those early days was the danger of Dad's work. Insulation procedures were still primitive; every now and then a lineman was electrocuted. Once I accompanied Mother and Dad to a home with the window blinds drawn in the middle of the day. My parents went inside while I hung about the yard: it was Dad who, once the current was shut down, had pulled the man from the wires.

If a minister was present at that funeral, I never heard about it. There must have been churches in the places where we lived, but I never recall going into one. Church was for people with new clothes and a pair of shoes for Sundays only.

Our moral training was based not on religion but on the distinction between "good people" and "bad people." Bad people were headed for a fate so awful that my parents could never bring themselves to describe it. Their misdeeds were shadowy affairs in my young mind too: drinking and playing cards and—most mysterious of all—"fooling around" with women. For the most part we were left to imagine both the crime and the punishment.

Good people, on the other hand, had a clear-cut arrangement of transgressions and penalties. Swearing, telling a lie, bringing home a bad report card—Dad would take his razor strap from the wall and haul the offender into a bedroom.

Usually it was me. Bertha Mae seemed to have been born good—quiet and hard-working—while Bob was too young to be suspected of originating the scrapes he and I got into. I was the one who was hauled, kicking, into the back room while Mother pleaded with Dad through the closed door. I'm sure Dad did not know how hard he whipped me; he was so strong that everything he did was exaggerated, and through the door I would hear Mother's sobs mingling with my own.

I'm also sure that his frustration played a part in his anger. The great Depression had settled over the country, striking hardest at growth industries like electricity. I was not aware, of course, of the nation's agony. I only knew that, unaccountably, there were no more pennies to be spent at the candy store.

Some of the boys in my fourth grade class still had money for gum. Each time the teacher's back was turned, the boy in the next aisle would produce an enormous pink bubble, then swallow it with a satisfying pop.

And still the weeks passed with never a penny left from Mother's market money. I don't even recall what I was looking for the day I found the Indian-head coins. Mother had sent me to fetch something from the dresser in her and Dad's bedroom. In the top drawer was the brown glass dish in which Mother kept her hairpins. And there, among the pins, were four Indian-head pennies. With the Depression a fever of coin collecting had swept the nation. Mother would compare each penny, nickel and dime which entered the house against the list in a little blue-backed pamphlet.

To me, however, these were simply the missing pennies from the grocery money. At last I had found them. I put them in my pocket and as soon as my chores at home were finished ran to the store and bought four bright-wrapped fruity-smelling balls of Bazooka bubble gum. I unwrapped the first one and read the comic before even leaving the store, then ran my tongue deliciously over the powdery pink surface.

By rewrapping the wad, I could nurse a single piece for several days. I had not even licked the sugar off the second piece when the theft was discovered. It was unthinkable that Bertha Mae could have done it, and Bob was too small to have seen into the top drawer, so I was summoned to the living room.

"Charles, did you take four pennies from your mother's pin dish?"

"No," I said, and promptly burst into tears.

That was the hardest whipping I ever received. Of course I carried the three unopened pieces of gum back to the store and got three pennies back, but not the precious Indian-heads. Worse than the welts on my backside was Mother's grief: she had convinced herself that those coins might bring $25 each.

We moved that summer to Enid, Oklahoma, to the tiny three-room house across from the elementary school. And it was here that I had my first good experience in a classroom. My fifth grade teacher, Miss Perry, was one of that astonishing race of spinster schoolteachers, of whom small-town America boasted thousands, whose whole life was dedicated to raising the sights of other people's children. It was her conviction, long before psychologists codified it, that each child, each year, must succeed at something.

I'm sure that in my case she looked long and hard. But by midyear she had found it:

"Your penstrokes, Charles!" She picked up the ruled paper on which I had been drawing connected loops. "They're so even and regular! I'm sure you could develop the best penmanship in the class. That is—" for Miss Perry was honest as well as kind, "among the boys."

After that I wore my pen point to a nub making the round slanting loops, each so like the other that at the end of the line a perfect cylinder had been formed down which, I liked to think, a bullet could fly and never touch the edges.

And now an even more exciting thing happened. Miss Perry entered a sheet of my penmanship exercises in a regional contest. For days I scarcely breathed with suspense. At last Miss Perry beckoned me to her desk.

"Charles! You've done it! You've won! Of all the fifth-grade boys in northwest Oklahoma you've taken the very first place!"

The schoolroom seemed to spin around me. First place! Me—Charles Blair—a winner!

There was a framed certificate, Miss Perry went on, to prove what I had done; the principal himself was going to present it to me in front of the whole school tomorrow. And then came the words that brought the spinning room to a sickening halt.

"The certificate is 75¢. Don't forget to bring it to the office first thing tomorrow morning!"

I kicked at the snow on our sagging front porch. How was I going to talk my parents out of that much money?

"Seventy-five cents for *what?*" Mother cried as I knew she would. "Just for making some squiggles on a piece of paper? Your father has worries enough without you bringing up any such foolishness."

I cried myself to sleep that night, and next morning got to school even before the teacher. "Miss Perry," I said when she appeared, "I don't guess I'll go to the office anyway, to pay for that certificate. I don't guess I really want it. I couldn't really use it for anything."

I could never lie without give-away tears. "Charles," said Miss Perry gently, "is it the money?"

I nodded, wishing the floor would open beneath me. Miss Perry was rummaging in her purse. "We went into this contest together, Charles." She pressed three quarters into my hand. "And we'll see it through together!"

And so I received my certificate, standing in front of the student body to be told that I had brought honor and credit to Jefferson Elementary. It was the most splendid moment I had ever known, and the most terrible. For it seemed to me that instead of admiration in the eyes turned to me, I saw contempt. *He didn't have the money!*—although there was no way they could have known. *He had to borrow from the teacher!*

I used to daydream about having lots of money. The downtown section of Enid was built around an open square with a bandshell where concerts were given in the summer. Shops faced the four sides of this square and I would spend hours mooning from one to the other. The windows at Kress's five-and-dime were good for a whole Saturday morning. But best of all was the hardware store, on the street level of a two-story building. The second floor was occupied by a domino parlor where, Mother informed me in a shuddering whisper, men gambled for money. I did not even allow my eyes to rise to those second-floor windows, for if Bad People existed anywhere in Enid it was certainly there. Downstairs, however, a plate-glass window extended almost to the sidewalk and just inside, leaning one against another, were the bicycles—red, blue, and green, their sunburst spokes flashing silver lights as I trailed back and forth.

By the sixth grade my need for a bicycle had become critical. Because there were no new electric lines going up, there was no reason to keep moving, and it looked as though our family was settling down at last. Dad took what part-time work he could find around Enid, mostly menial jobs like cleaning furnaces. A lineman working at the top of the tall poles was a heroic figure, but this ash-covered specter turning stooped and weary onto our front porch—the whole school must know that my father was the man who swept out their cellars.

To make my self-consciousness more acute, it was this year that I discovered girls. One girl, to be exact, a golden-haired, green-eyed 11-year-old named Claudia whose father owned the bookstore on the town square. The problem was that only the boys with bicycles had much luck in attracting the attention of any girl. Circling the playground with no hands, taking the high curb in front of the school without dismounting—these were what drew stares of admiration.

Which is why I was disbelieving when Claudia Williams, the prettiest girl in the class, allowed me to walk her to her house one day. It was a very large house in the "nice" section of town, literally on the other side of the tracks from ours. The Rock Island Railroad ran through Enid; working-class houses like ours were east of the tracks, the homes of store owners and professional people to the west. They were two separate worlds and I don't think it ever occurred to my parents to try to cross into that other realm, or to want to.

But I walked at Claudia's side down the tree-shaded streets like a soul newly admitted to heaven. Here the houses had grass in their yards and flower gardens instead of vegetables. I wanted—oh, I wanted so badly—to belong to this world, and after that I walked Claudia home every day she would let me.

My one terror was that we would encounter her father and that he would recognize me as the boy who came into the bookstore with his mother at the start of each term to apply for state assistance. Textbooks and supplies at that time were supplied by the government only if a student could not afford them. What if Mr. Williams saw me with his daughter and told her I was the boy who could not even pay for his own pencils!

And then one lovely spring afternoon, three blocks from Claudia's house, something even worse occurred. Down the sidewalk behind us came Duke Everett on his red bicycle. Duke was the son of Enid's dentist, a citizen of this grassy, leafy neighborhood where I was only an intruder, and he sounded his two-tone horn as though he owned the place.

"Give you a ride, Claudia," he said when we had jumped aside.

And Claudia, without a backward glance at me, climbed onto the crossbar of his bicycle and let him pedal her out of my life.

The tears I could never control dribbled down my cheeks as I trudged back to our dusty street on the wrong side of the tracks. But behind the tears was something else. It was the resolve I had felt forming in me the week before when Duke Everett caught me with the milk pail. Somehow, someway I was going to *make* people look up to me. I'd ride a bike and drink milk out of bottles and when I needed a pencil I'd just slap my money down on Mr. Williams' counter, and everybody would have to respect me.

Only—how did I start? I couldn't be a dentist or a store owner till I grew up. One job I saw boys doing was selling newspapers down in the town square—some of them not much older than I was. It took me a week to get up the courage to ask one of them how you got a job like that. He took me around the corner to the newspaper office where a man in shirtsleeves looked me over.

"You're small for your age," the man said approvingly, as though this were something to be proud of. "And your toes are coming out of your shoes, and you look scared to death. People like that."

I didn't know what he was talking about. But that September, 1932, the day after my twelfth birthday, I started selling the Enid *Daily Eagle* each afternoon after school. There was a rigid hierarchy in the locations assigned by Mr. Campbell. The best station of all was the curb in front of the Youngblood Hotel, a block from the square, a modern ten-story building boasting an elevator, the pride of the town. Next best was outside the Oxford Hotel, older and smaller and less expensive. The third choice was the sidewalk in front of J.C. Penney's Department Store and then any other location on the square. I took up a post in front of Kress's, across the square from Penney's.

Perhaps because I was small and frightened-looking, as Mr. Campbell said, I did well from the start. Customers became regulars, and often along with the nickel which the paper cost would come a pat on the head and a penny or two for myself. All of the money, both my commission on each paper and my tips, went of course into the family coffer. It never occurred to me not to turn over the contents of my pockets to Mother each evening, any more than it occurred to her to thank me for doing so. This was the way families like ours did it: each working for all. Bertha Mae, at the top of her eleventh-grade class, corrected papers after school for the teachers, and even eight-year-old Bob found odd jobs for the neighbors.

So though I was bringing home 30 or 40¢ a day the dream of a bicycle was as remote as ever. In March, 1933, Mr. Campbell promoted me to the number-three spot outside Penney's and the following fall, when I'd been selling papers for a year, he moved me to the Oxford. In that location I'd be back in his office three or four times an afternoon for a fresh bundle of papers; by that second Christmas I'd been given the coveted corner outside the Youngblood Hotel.

Now indeed my sights soared, for here I was literally on the threshhold of another world. More even than the increased earnings, the new location was, for me, a revelation of the world. Names of faraway places fell from the lips of the men who passed through these doors. My childish rivalry with the likes of Duke Everett was laid aside as I hung on these conversations. Who cared about the fashionable section of Enid—I was going to see Tulsa, Wichita, Oklahoma City!

Occasionally when I could not make change I would follow a customer into the hotel lobby, and there, while he went to the front desk, I would all but hold my breath. To the left was the shining tile and chrome coffee shop, where people sat at a round counter on stools anchored to the floor. And sure enough, there at the back, was the elevator with a button in the wall to make it come.

In the evenings, at home, I tried to describe these marvels. The others weren't hostile to what I reported, or jealous of the people who lived that way, they were just totally, deeply indifferent. I thought nine-year-old Bob would at least be interested in the elevator, but he was as incurious as the others, and gradually I stopped trying to bring that other world into our little frame house.

My job, in fact, was separating me in many ways from my family. The very amount of money I was earning was a barrier. Many afternoons I pocketed two, three, even four dollars. Dad was bringing home $12 a week from his long days cleaning furnaces. When spring, 1934, arrived, even that regular source of income ceased; many weeks he made nothing. How could I, not yet 14, hand Mother more than he did?

There was a small shelf on the wall of the tiny bedroom I shared with Bob. There was no hallway in our house and Mother and Dad had to walk through this room on the way to theirs. Still I could think of no more private place to hide my astonishing earnings, and day after day I would put a dollar or more in nickels and dimes up there in an empty Post Toasties box.

On days when papers sold badly I would take some of this money out to feed into the family economy without embarrassing Dad. Still the secret cache grew. There was over $30 in it the day my mother, in a frenzy of spring cleaning, cleared off the shelf and discovered it. I knew when I saw her face that something was wrong.

"Charles! In the box—all that money! Oh Charles, did you. . . ." I could see it was a struggle for her even to say the word *steal*.

"It's all mine, Mother! Honest! I earned it, all of it! I was saving it to give to you."

My words sounded unconvincing even to me.

"Oh Charles, Charles," Mother moaned. "When your father comes home—"

"Don't tell him, Mother! Please, don't tell him!" Dad would

reach for the strap first, listen to explanations later. "If you'll just wait, I can prove I didn't steal it!"

But how? How does a person prove what he did *not* do?

"I'll get my boss to come here," I said recklessly. "He'll tell you I earned it! Just don't tell Dad tonight!"

And so the following evening Mr. Campbell accompanied me to our three-room home. I suffered agonies thinking how we must appear to him, sitting with his hat in his hand on the day-couch that was also Bertha Mae's bed. But he seemed not to notice. "Charlie's my very best salesman," he assured my parents warmly. "You can be sure he's earned that money. Of course in his location he gets good tips too."

At last my mother and father seemed convinced. Relief flooded their faces at the assurance that their son was not a thief. Relief and something else too. A kind of withdrawal, a backing away from a world they could not enter. With Mr. Campbell's visit the gulf between us grew wider still.

When summer vacation came I began hanging around the Youngblood Hotel most of the day, even before the paper appeared. And that was how, one morning, I came to be invited upstairs. Mr. Hawthorne was a shoe salesman who came often through Enid. I'd sold him a paper a number of times and now, seeing me standing about with nothing to do, he asked me if I'd come up to his showroom and shine up the samples he had on display.

The room where he met with buyers was only on the second floor and to my disappointment we climbed the stairs rather than taking the elevator. But the display was wonderful. On tables around the walls he had set out dozens of new shoes smelling intoxicatingly of leather. Nowadays we bought our shoes from the barrel in the secondhand clothing store, and when the soles wore through we put cardboard in them. Mother bought Post Toasties cereal because the cardboard in their boxes was strongest.

With a soft rag I rubbed every shoe till it shone. Mr. Hawthorne must have been pleased because he handed me a dollar bill, the most money I'd ever earned at one time. He was watching me with a curious expression.

"Say!" he said suddenly, "have you had breakfast?"

I hadn't. Mr. Hawthorne said he hadn't either, so back down the stairs we went and—wonder of wonders—we were going into the coffee shop! I climbed onto the stool next to Mr. Hawthorne's, heart hammering for fear I would do something wrong. I picked up the menu at my place as he had done, and pretended to study it, though the words danced in front of me.

"The pancakes look good to me," he said.

"They look good to me too."

In a few moments the waitress, smart in a white apron that came only to her waist, set in front of us two stacks of steaming, golden-brown cakes, mounds of butter melting on the top. I copied Mr. Hawthorne's every move. With his knife he smoothed the butter over the cakes. Then he reached for the can of syrup: "Help yourself. I have to stay away from sugar."

I had never seen anything so beautiful as that can, shaped like a little log house with the chimney forming the spout. I had no idea how to use it, though, so I shook my head.

"I have to stay away from it too."

Those buttery pancakes were the most delicious things I'd ever tasted. I drew out each bite, wanting the enchanted moment to last forever, sitting at this gleaming tile counter wiping my mouth with a paper napkin that would just be tossed away when we were through. Someday I was going to eat in restaurants and toss money onto the counter as Mr. Hawthorne was doing now. "Keep the change," he told the waitress. *Keep the change,* I repeated to myself, practicing.

Only . . . I'd been selling newspapers for nearly two years now, and was as far as ever from having that bicycle. Perhaps by keeping out a few pennies a day I could, by now, have accumulated the unthinkable sum of $44.95 for the racing model my heart was set on. But how could I justify such a thing at home? Legs were made for getting us from place to place, Mother was fond of observing.

And then one momentous evening, sitting beside Dad as he

performed the nightly ritual of checking the help-wanted ads in the *Eagle,* my answer jumped out at me. There were few jobs being offered in late summer, 1934, and those that did appear were all too familiar. Either the pay was too low, or the applicant had to be single, or the schooling required was more than Dad had had. So when a new ad appeared in that all-too-short column, it fairly leaped off the page.

> DELIVERY BOY Stunkle Drugs. After school and weekends. Must own bicycle and be familiar city streets. Apply in person 8 a.m.-6 p.m.

Must own . . . why, a bicycle would be as necessary as Dad's climbing hooks! Long before eight the following morning I was standing outside Stunkle's Drug Store two blocks from the square. At last I saw Mr. Stunkle coming.

"What's this? A job applicant already?" He glanced up and down the deserted sidewalk. "Do you have a bike son? The boy who takes this job has to have a bike."

"Yes sir! Uh—no sir. I mean, I know, and I'm planning to get a bicycle right away."

He let the two of us into the small cluttered shop and raised the window shades. "Haven't I seen you selling newspapers around town? I'm sure you're making more than I can pay."

He was looking down at me quizically, a tall, grey-bearded man; and suddenly I found myself telling him about my long and hopeless yearning for a bicycle.

"Well now," he said, "let's see how well you know this town. How would you get from here to 614 Maple Street?"

I was silent.

He tried me with several other addresses, all in the "good" part of town where his delivery customers lived, and I failed them all.

"But I'll find out where they are, Mr. Stunkle! I'll go up and down those streets till I know every house! Please, Mr. Stunkle!"

At last he agreed to give me a try. Two more hurdles remained: to persuade my parents to let me switch to the lower-paying job and to talk the hardware store into selling me the bicycle on credit.

The store was the easier part. The eight dollars a week which the delivery job paid was less than half what I'd been making selling papers, but it was a fixed salary and Mr. Stunkle's name was respected. If I put down the two weeks' salary which Mr. Stunkle would advance me, and agreed to pay $1.25 a week thereafter for 27 weeks, I could take the bicycle from the store today.

As I ran home I could almost feel the handlebars between my fingers. But convincing my parents was something else. The loss of family income was a frightening prospect, only partly offset by the discount Mr. Stunkle allowed employees on medicines and supplies. An even more serious objection was that the new job would put me on the streets after dark. What dreadful things transpired "after dark" I could only imagine, except that it was then that Bad People practiced their badness.

It was after the drug store closed at six, however, that Mr. Stunkle made up his prescriptions, and delivery "up till 8:00 p.m." was one of the proud slogans of his service. It was still light at eight o'clock at this time of year, I reminded Dad and Mother, and when the days grew shorter, well, by then I'd be 14, and on my bicycle I could outrace whatever Bad People were about.

At last, more in exhaustion than conviction, they said yes. My feet barely touched the ground as I raced back to give Mr. Stunkle the news, then to the square with the $16 down payment on my bicycle. I wheeled it out of the hardware store scarcely sure it was really happening, I had played this scene so often in my mind. Out into the late summer sunshine, ease the wheels gently off the curb. Left foot on the pedal, swing the other over and settle onto the sleek black leather seat. For years I'd begged the loan of other boys' bikes in the playground. But this lean metal beauty was my own and the wind in my ears sounded like cheering.

From that day on, earning money became an obsession. I

ran errands for our delivery customers, I swept out their garages, I mowed their lawns. Most of this additional money went home, of course, along with my salary, but occasionally, on good days, I could put a little aside for the accessories beckoning on the shelves of the hardware store.

The kickstand was a huge step up; now the bike no longer had to lean servilely against a tree or a building. I traded the round reflector for a diamond-shaped one, then drilled holes in the fender to hold additional ones. Grandest of all was when I discarded the painted fender altogether for one made of chrome. With a canvas bag proclaiming Stunkle Drugs over my shoulder I would flash through the streets of Enid, scattering sunlight from a dozen silver surfaces. I often made deliveries on Claudia's street, and occasionally saw her on the sidewalk. I never even slowed down.

All through ninth, tenth and eleventh grade I delivered drugs for Mr. Stunkle. We were no longer living in the three-room bungalow across from the elementary school. We had moved to a two-story house on Third Street, around the corner from Southwestern Bible College. Students from the college rented the upstairs bedrooms, making it possible for us to afford the house.

But the yearning to see the world, planted by scraps of conversation at the Youngblood Hotel, had never left me. When in the spring of my junior year the help-wanted column listed a job selling magazine subscriptions door to door with "opportunity to travel," I was once again the first applicant on the scene.

The man who opened the door on the third floor of the Oxford Hotel introduced himself as the representative of *Wichita Eagle*, a daily morning newspaper with subscribers all over southern Kansas and northern Oklahoma. Although salesmen would indeed, as the ad had said, offer subscriptions to both *Liberty Magazine* and *Collier's*, the real competition was between the Wichita paper and the big dailies from Tulsa and Oklahoma City.

"I know I can do it, Mr. White! I know I can sell the *Eagle!*"

I described my newspaper-hawking days. "You can ask Mr. Campbell how many I sold!"

Mr. White looked unconvinced. "Selling a $15 subscription is different from making a nickel sale on the street. Do you have any idea how hard it is to get people to spend $15 nowadays?"

"Yes sir," I said with feeling.

"You have to go to their homes, and you have to look presentable." His eyes traveled over my hand-me-down clothes. "You'd have to wear a suit. All our salesmen do. Do you own a suit?"

"I was planning on buying one."

"You couldn't walk up to someone's door in those shoes either. You'd have to wear your best ones and make sure they were shined."

I didn't tell him that the shoes on my feet were the only pair I owned, and I wrung from him the promise of a two-week trial period as soon as school let out in May. It was now the beginning of March. Ten weeks in which to convince my family and somehow, someway get hold of new shoes and a suit.

At first of course my parents said no. What they could not accept was the thought of my being away from home overnight. As salesmen fanned out through small towns in the area they would often not return to Enid until the weekend. I reminded them that "the men" — Mr. White's phrase — worked only in pairs. "So you see, Mother, nothing could possibly happen."

"But what kind of men are they?" she worried. "What do we know about them?

In the end, I believed, the promise of increased earnings would win my parents over. Meantime I had already picked out my suit down at Davis Clothing Store. It was a dignified black one, "Oxford grey" Mr. Davis called it, and—marvel of marvels—it came with a vest. There could have been no worse choice for the dusty roads of an Oklahoma summer, but I was not thinking in mundane terms. I pictured myself buttoning that vest, perhaps slipping one hand into a trouser pocket.

It cost $12 and Mr. Davis agreed to put a SOLD sign on it if I gave him two dollars down and agreed to bring in a dollar a week. Each time I picked up an order at Stunkle's I would ride through the square, to make sure my suit was still in the window.

It took every spare minute before school and Sundays to earn the dollar I gave Mr. Davis each week. How would I ever set aside another $4 for shoes? May was almost here and Mr. White would be coming back to Enid. How could I show up again in these old shoes with their Post Toasties soles?

I found myself haunting the shoe department at J.C. Penney's. It was at the back of the store, beside the stairs that led up to the mezzanine where the credit department and other offices were. I went up and asked if I could have the shoes now and pay for them later, as I had the bicycle.

"A charge account, you mean? Are you 18? You have to be 18 to open an account."

I wasn't. Wouldn't be for four more months.

And so I came into the shoe department simply to look. There were chairs where people could sit while they tried on the shoes, and little stools where the salesman sat in front of them. Once I sat down in one of these chairs, just pretending. But a clerk came up just as though I were a customer.

"Yes sir. What can I show you today?"

From his pocket he drew what looked like a wooden ruler with turned-up ends. Dragging a stool in front of my chair, he placed this ruler on the floor. "If you'll just stand up, sir, we'll get you measured."

I stood up, realizing I was to put my foot on that wooden thing.

"Without the shoe," he prompted me.

Blushing furiously I took it off. Surely when he saw the cardboard inside he'd know that I was not really going to make a purchase. But he brought a stack of boxes from the shelves and opened them with a flourish.

Everything about the experience intoxicated me. The tissue

paper inside the boxes, the little piece of metal with which he eased the shoes over my heel. At last he drew from the box the most beautiful pair of shoes I had ever seen. They had no laces, only a strap with a small metal buckle that was only for looks, because he did not unfasten it. The shoe slipped over my foot as though it had been made for me alone. I put on the other one too, then stood up and walked a little way on the soft carpet. A mirror reflected them back at me: dark brown, gleaming. The hardest thing I had ever done was to sit down and let him pull those shoes off me.

"They fit you nicely."

"Yes. Well, I—I'll think about it."

He dropped the shoes back into their box and began gathering the stack together. I stood up to leave. But I could not take my eyes off the box that held those shoes. The clerk was carrying the stack back to the shelves, putting the boxes in their places.

And as I watched him, the entire plan appeared in my head.

Every detail was there, even to the proper time to do it. I knew it would be stealing, but nothing, not the memory of the Indian-head pennies, not Mother's lectures of Dad's razor strap, was as strong as my desire for those shoes. The time to do it was Friday evening after the workers at the Champlain Oil Refinery were paid. That night the stores were crowded and many added part-time clerks.

At 6:30 p.m. Friday I parked my bike on the sidewalk outside Penney's and joined the crowd pushing through the doors. Just inside I stopped and rolled my sleeves above the elbow, turning them twice the way clerks did. Then I walked back to the shoe department. I glanced at the stock shelves to make sure the box holding "my" pair was still there, then scanned the railing around the mezzanine level to make sure no store official was watching. In the shoe department every chair was occupied, all the clerks busy. I waited until the one who had helped me was bent over a customer, then stepped to the shelves, picked up my box and carried it briskly to the wrapping desk. From the long roll of paper beneath the counter I tore off a piece and folded it neatly around the box. I broke off a length of string from the spindle on the countertop, deftly tied my parcel, and walked away. Near the front door I rolled down my sleeves, then sauntered out to the sidewalk, a customer with a purchase beneath his arm.

When Mr. White returned to Enid the following week I appeared at his hotel room wearing those brown buckle shoes and a three-piece suit with price tags tucked out of sight but still in place. I had never owned a piece of clothing with store tags on it; they seemed too wonderful to cut off and throw away.

I had a bad moment when I saw the other sales recruits. Not one was under 20 and several were married with families to feed. Jobs were still so scarce in Oklahoma, that spring of '38, that grown men were competing for jobs with high school kids. Mr. White signed us all up, though, on a see-how-you-do basis. I was teamed with the next youngest man, a 20-year-old named Fred. Mr. White piled six of us into his long black Packard. He dropped Fred and me off outside the town of Cherokee, with instructions to canvass Jet, Nashville and Pond Creek before returning at the end of the week to Enid. Each of us carried sample copies of *Collier's* and *Liberty* magazines along with the morning's *Wichita Eagle*.

"Don't fool with that end of town," Mr. White waved away a neighborhood of unpainted frame homes. "Go to houses with telephone lines. Say something nice about the kid if there is one. If you ask for a drink of water it sometimes gets you inside."

But the better-off citizens of Cherokee were not buying subscriptions that day, nor were the few cars on the highway stopping for hitchhikers as we trudged to the next town. Although we drank gallons of water and complimented dozens of little boys and girls, by the end of the day we had sold one subscription to *Collier's*, one to *Liberty*, and none at all to the *Eagle*.

When evening came, we looked, as we'd been instructed, for the words "Sleeping Rooms," in the window of a private home. Giving 25¢ each to the housewife, we crawled together into a double bed that nearly filled a small upstairs bedroom. I had shared a bed with my brother all my life; only as Fred broke into a startling series of snorts and whistles did I begin to appreciate Bob as a bedfellow.

This was the first night I had ever spent away from home. Outside on this May evening it was still daylight. I lay on my side listening to Fred gasp and gargle, watching some fluffs of dust chase each other across the floor. That was something else I only now realized: no matter how shabby the houses we had lived in, I had never seen a speck of dust in my mother's home.

Next day was the same: up three steps onto a wooden porch, ring the doorbell. "Good morning, m'am. That's a bright-looking boy you have there."

Already, this early in the year, the unpaved roads had turned to dust. Soon my handkerchief was black from wiping my shoes at each doorstep. In every direction the road stretched to the horizon without a curve or a tree to break the shimmering haze of heat. By the end of the second day I had discarded my vest, carrying it folded beneath the magazines. On our best day we sold four subscriptions.

At the end of the week we caught a ride back to Enid in the cab of a cattle truck. Mr. White was not in his room at the Oxford Hotel. A note on the door instructed salesmen to report to him at the domino parlor above the hardward store.

"Come on, what are you waiting for?" Fred asked, tense because of the poor results we had to show.

But a hand seemed to have closed around my chest at the words *domino parlor*. "You go on and report, Fred. I ought to go home."

"Oh no you don't! We go together, and if we get fired, we get fired together."

And so I trailed after him up the stairs. As Fred pushed open the door the clatter of dominoes slapped onto slate table tops struck my ears. It took us a while to pick out Mr. White through the cigar smoke stinging our eyes. He did not look up from the table as we made our report, nor glance at the thin pile of subscriptions forms Fred laid before him. From a stack of bills on the table he counted out ten dollars for each of us.

"Another week like this, you're both out," were the only words he spoke.

Monday morning he drove us 70 miles north to a small town just over the Kansas border. As the Packard disappeared into the water mirage already shimmering over the highway, Fred and I held a council of desperation.

"We've got to sell the *Eagle!*"

"But how?" I put in hopelessly.

"If there were some way to make people feel sorry for us," Fred pressed on. "What if we said one of our mothers was sick and—no, everyone uses that."

We started aimlessly down a street of small, neat homes, "I've got it!" he shouted. He took the stack of papers and magazines I was carrying. "Let your arms hang limp," he instructed. "Put your head on one side. Like that. No, let your mouth hang open."

At last he had me arranged to his satisfaction. "Don't you see! You're my younger brother, only there's something wrong with you and I've got to get treatment for you!" He rehearsed me a while longer until he felt we were ready. "Only not here, in case someone was watching."

Three miles down the road we put our "idiot brother" act in motion. At the first few houses I was so terrified I'm sure I really looked feeble-minded. Every house took at least one subscription, and one lady was so moved by my plight that she took the *Eagle* and both magazines.

After that I lost my fear and was less convincing, but under Fred's coaching I gradually became a very passable idiot, and out sales soared. Mr. White was so startled by the results of our second week's efforts that he actually looked up from his domino game. From being his least productive team we were almost on a par with his best.

In fact, by early July it was Fred and I, along with two older men, who were chosen from the Enid area to attend the

Eagle's annual sales awards banquet in Wichita. For days I was in a lather of excitement, brushing and pressing my Oxford-grey suit, polishing my shoes until I nearly rubbed the leather off.

The four winning salesmen met Mr. White at the Oxford Hotel on Saturday noon for the 120-mile drive north. We were to spend the night at his home, following the banquet, and as we reached the outskirts of Wichita he told us, "We'll stop by the house first so you can freshen up and change."

I'd be glad to get out of the back seat where the hot summer wind whipped my face, but what we were to "change" I could not imagine. Mr. White took us into a living room where the sofa and chairs matched, like in the furniture store window on the square. Mrs. White came in, walking on little high-heeled shoes that showed her toes. Her yellow hair was piled in curls on the top of her head and her mouth was pink. Her eyes, however, were blazing. She didn't even glance at the four of us.

"You stupid jerk!" she shouted at Mr. White through those pink lips. "Took your little trick across the state line this time, didn't you? Well, the police have been looking for you, and if you think—"

Mr. White was gesturing frantically. "Not here, Millie! Not in front of the men!"

"C'mon," Fred said, "let's get our stuff."

We shuffled awkwardly out of the room and escaped to the outdoors. I could make no sense at all of Mrs. White's outburst. From the trunk of the Packard Fred and the others took suitcases and I realized that they had brought extra clothes with them and that that was what we were to "change."

When we got back the Whites were no longer in the living room, though from somewhere in the house we could still hear her screaming at him. "I guess we're supposed to go in here," one of the men said, pushing open the door to a downstairs bedroom. While Fred and the others put on fresh clothes, I smoothed my jacket and trousers on the bed as I did each night in the sleeping rooms. Soon Mr. White rapped on the door.

"All set, men? We'd better get going!"

No reference was made to the astonishing scene in the living room and I soon forgot it in the thrill of seeing downtown Wichita. In my farthest flights of fancy, I had never imagined so many buildings, so many lights. The banquet was held in the ballroom of the Allis Hotel, and all in one moment my fantasy world, which till then had been defined by the lobby and coffee shop of the Youngblood Hotel, took on a vast new dimension.

Mr. White went forward to join the other district managers at a long table set on a platform, while we found four places at one of the round tables that filled the rest of the room. I could scarcely eat for gazing around me. There was an incredible amount of silverware on our table: two forks and two spoons at every place and a little knife on a small plate just large enough to hold one roll. Most amazing of all, the table itself was hidden beneath a white cloth, so spotless that I was terrified lest something fall off my plate and touch it.

When the dessert dishes had been cleared away one of the men at the head table rose from his chair. "Max Levine," the man beside me whispered, "Owner of the *Eagle*."

First, Mr. Levine thanked us all for coming. Then he started speaking about his own life. He had been poor as a boy, he said, but in his heart had been a desire to be better than he was. He described how he felt when people made fun of his clothes, the house he lived in, his way of talking. I listened open-mouthed. This great man could have been me!

When Mr. Levine talked about how he had achieved success, I all but stopped breathing to hear. Hard work, he said. Regular habits. No drinking. No loose living. But . . . my father had lived that way all his life and he was still sweeping cellars.

On the drive back to Enid the next day I was silent, trying to sort out the confusion in my mind. The confusion grew at the end of that week when Fred and I climbed the stairs to the domino parlor and discovered that Mr. White was not at his table.

"You come around asking for him again," the owner of the parlor told us, "and I'll break your back."

"What's he so angry about?" I gasped as we scrambled down the stairs.

"And how do we collect our commissions?" asked Fred, more practically.

At the Oxford Hotel there was a message from the circulation manager of the *Eagle*: Mr. White's replacement would arrive on Monday. The new district manager turned out to be a brisk, efficient young man who drove an antique Ford touring car. He never spoke about Mr. White, but among the salesmen the sensational news circulated: Mr. White was in jail.

Over the next weeks other details passed from mouth to mouth. Mr. White had gone to Kansas with the wife of the man who ran the domino parlor; because they had crossed a state line the charge was kidnapping, a federal offense. For months I could not pass beneath those second-story windows without a chill sliding down my spine. Everything Mother and Dad had told me was true! Men who played dominoes came to a bad end.

The new manager announced that when salesmen were in Enid during the week we were to remain together, maintaining what he called "morale." He took a row of rooms on the third floor of the Oxford for the use of any teams that were in town. They were small and dark, but better than the "sleeping rooms" with their outdoor toilets. At night we gathered under the lightbulb in the hotel corridor while the others pitched pennies at a crack in the floorboards. Mr. White's fate was still too fresh for me to risk taking part in gambling, but I would watch from the sidelines and occasionally be called upon to arbitrate a throw.

This is what I was doing the night my life changed forever.

Something was different about that evening right from the start. Ordinarily the game proceeded in kind of a stupor of boredom; tonight the guys whooped and shouted and slapped each other on the back. There was some whispering at the end of the hall near the stairs and then:

"Here they come!"

Up the stairway came five young women—or, not so young. Even in the dim light of the corridor I could see the thick powder, the impossibly long lashes. I knew in that first paralyzing moment that these were "the wrong kind of women" that Dad had warned of.

Fred had slipped his arm around one of them and was fumbling with our room key. Other couples were forming, drifting toward other rooms. There was only one stairway on the floor and I bolted for it, though it meant pressing past the giggling pairs.

"Hey honey, don't go away!" one of the women called.

I rounded the landing on the second floor and plunged down the final flight like a man pursued. Out in the warm night air I kept running. Down to the square, past Penney's and the hardware store, dodging around the ominous rectangle of light from the domino parlor above, till at last I stopped, panting, in front of the shaded windows of Stunkle's drug store.

With hands that shook I lit a cigarette. For over a year I'd been smoking, rolling my own from a pack of Bull Durham tobacco, as Dad did. It was eight o'clock, downtown Enid shuttered and silent. I finished the cigarette and roamed back to the square, then drifted down a side street. How long did—women like that, how long did they stay? I was returning to the square with a half-formed idea of spending the night in the bandstand, when far down another street I noticed a light.

A few blocks further I saw that it was a spotlight on a parking lot filled with cars. In the center of the lot was a large new wooden building with a curved roof; piles of lumber and a cement mixer stood near by.

From inside I heard music, but when I peered through the door, I saw only a bare wooden vestibule. From an inner door came the sound of a piano and a woman's voice singing. Uncertainly I crossed the vestibule and eased open the inner door. Three or four hundred people were sitting on wooden benches in a large, unfinished room with a tarpaper ceiling. On a platform down front a grey-haired lady was singing with her eyes closed, while a man accompanied her on a piano.

When the lady finished singing nobody clapped. The man got up from the piano and said that now Sister Buffum was going to sing a song he himself had written. I wanted very much to stay in this cheerful lighted place filled with people. There were no empty benches near the back so I simply stayed where I was in the doorway. The words of the next song were about prayer, and I realized, standing there, that for the first time in my life I was inside a church. Somehow it wasn't at all what I thought a church would be like. Mother always said that church was for the rich, but these people didn't look any different from anyone else.

The second song ended and Sister Buffum and the piano player stepped down off the platform. A young man got up from the front row, jumped onto the platform, and stood looking out at the people. I supposed that he was going to sing too, but instead he began to speak, striding from one end of the platform to the other as he did. He looked to be in his late twenties, tall, athletic-looking, and—talking about me!

"You came here tonight because you were tired of wandering and finding no rest."

It was true.

"You knew you could not go back to the place you came from, and yet you knew of no other place to go."

How could he have known! As he continued to walk briskly up and down, I realized that he was not only talking about me, he was talking to me. There was no one else in the room, only myself and this energetic man who knew all about me.

"There are things in your life that cause you to blush, things you must keep secret. There is deceit in your life, falsehood, dissimulation." I saw myself as the idiot brother, limping up to some unsuspecting household.

"This very night you have looked into the face of evil. You have fled it, yet you suspect it is only waiting, biding its time."

My throat was dry, my heart hammering.

"Friends, family, none can avail. Indeed it is in your own home that you feel most alone. A stranger to your kin."

He stopped in the center of the platform. "Oh friend, do you long for peace, for an end to running?"

I did!

"There is One who can give you that peace. His name is Jesus. He is calling you now. Calling you to come. To cast your burden of fear and guilt on Him. Oh friend, come!"

The speaker's arms opened wide. His eyes looked straight into mine. "It is no accident that you are here tonight. You thought it was by chance, but it was His love, drawing you. You thought you had to earn love, by impressing people. But love is yours right now! Tonight! Come! Take love!"

Here and there men and women were getting up from the benches and coming down to where the young man stood. In front of the platform a long board had been laid across some uprights, making a railing, and in front of that was a strip of carpet. People were getting down on their knees on that carpet.

"Son?"

I was surprised to see Sister Buffum standing in front of me. "Son," she said again, "I see that you are not saved."

I stared at her stupidly, wondering what she could be talking about. *Saved*? She was staring at my shirt. I looked down, but there was only the pouch of Bull Durham sticking out of my pocket.

"Don't you want to go forward?" she asked.

Yes I did—oh, so badly! But I didn't know what you were supposed to do.

"I'll go with you, if that will make it easier," Sister Buffum said.

I looked at her broad grandmotherly face.

"Yes, please," I said.

So we walked together down to the strip of carpet. She lowered herself slowly to her knees and I dropped down beside her. And suddenly I knew I was going to cry. I was nearly 18 years old and I hadn't cried since Claudia rode away on Duke Everett's bicycle. But they were falling now, big babyish tears sliding down my face and splashing onto the wooden railing. I wiped them hastily away, but more came, and there was something strange about them. Instead of rage that had always before come with tears, these felt—all right. More than all right! They felt good. *I* felt good. Happy. Crazily, impossibly happy!

And the happier I felt the harder I cried. I couldn't understand it. I knelt there next to Sister Buffum, tears dripping onto the wood, while inside I wasn't crying at all. I was singing and jumping and dancing for joy.

I felt hands on top of my head. "Father, we thank You for these tears." It was the young speaker. "We thank You that You are washing this child of Yours clean of every sin, every evil act and thought."

Why—that was exactly what it felt like! Like the tears were water and the water was washing away everything wrong.

"Say with me, son," the man said, his hands warm on my head, "I confess . . . "

"I confess . . . "

" . . . the wrong I have done. I ask You to forgive my sins . . . "

" . . . the wrong I have done and I ask you to forgive my sins."

"I thank You for dying on the cross for my atonement and rising again for my salvation."

I repeated the strange, difficult words, understanding none of them, feeling only the wild new joy rising inside me.

The hands lifted from my head, the young man moved to the person next to me. Sister Buffum stood up and I stood up too. At a bench she stepped back to let me sit down, but I never stopped walking. I crossed the vestibule in three steps, and raced out into the soft night air.

For a long time I walked the silent streets—but what a difference from an hour ago! Then I'd been confused and scared. Now I walked because of the singing inside me. I felt free, light. I wanted to run, so I did for several blocks. I wanted to jump, and I did that too. I had no name for the feeling pulsing through my veins, I only knew if I held still I would burst. When I finally returned to the Oxford Hotel, Fred was alone in our room, his snores audible clear down the hallway.

Next morning I woke to a brand new world. The district manager piled the same teams into the same Ford car and drove us to a wide place in the road no different from any other prairie town. It was mid-August, dust blanketed everything. But today even the overalls flapping on the clotheslines were beautiful.

"I don't want to do the idiot business," I told Fred.

"Okay, I'll do it today." Occasionally to relieve the monotony we swapped roles.

"No, I mean—" How could I tell Fred what had happened the night before, when I didn't know, myself? I only knew that the idiot brother with his head lolling to the side belonged to a life I had lived a very long time ago.

"Let's just show them the paper and the magazines," I said to Fred. "I mean, living way out here, I think they'd enjoy getting this paper."

And maybe because I believed it, we sold as many subscriptions that day without our act as with it. By the end of a three-day circuit, in fact, our sales were up, and Fred was elated.

To my delight, the night we got back to Enid, that parking lot was again full of cars, the round-roofed building more crowded than ever. Sister Buffum greeted me like a long-lost son. She told me that the speaker—only she said "preacher"—was named Lloyd Johnson, and that he was in Enid for only four weeks, holding these church services every night in what she called a "revival." Now that I knew he was a stranger I was even more amazed that he had known so much about me. When I mentioned this to Sister Buffum she said, "That's the Holy Spirit," as if that should explain it.

There were 12 more nights of meetings and I started thinking up reasons why Fred and I had to keep getting back to Enid. Fred was puzzled, because we'd never done so well on the road, but I couldn't get enough of sitting in that unfinished building with its tarpaper roof, hearing Sister Buffum sing and listening to Mr. Johnson preach. One night he talked about what to do when the revival ended.

"Every day read your Bible. And every night, before you go to sleep, get down on your knees beside your bed and pray for at least 20 minutes."

Here were problems indeed. He talked about reading the Bible as though of course everybody had one. And indeed I seemed to be the only one there who was not carrying one. Sister Buffum spoke about it one night. "I see you don't bring your Bible to service, Brother Blair," she said.

"I don't have a Bible," I said.

"Don't have a Bible!" She sounded so shocked that I realized I had said something shameful. But the next evening Sister Buffum gave me a beautiful Bible with a real leather cover and gold edges on the tops of the pages.

Getting down on my knees beside my bed was another matter. Weeknights Fred and I shared a bed, either in a sleeping room or at the Oxford, and on weekends I still slept with Bob. How could I explain to them what I was doing on my knees? A single room at the Oxford cost two dollars extra each night, but out in the small towns a single sleeping room cost only 40¢ instead of 25¢. So I told Fred that when we were away from Enid I wanted my own room. He thought it was because of the snoring and got mad, but it didn't matter much because I had to start my last year of high school in about three weeks and he'd have to find another partner anyway.

It was a strange feeling, the first night I closed the door and found myself alone—the first time I'd ever had a bedroom to myself. There was a metal bed with a cornhusk mattress, a washbowl and pitcher on a small stand, a single chair. I hung my suit jacket on the nail behind the door, lifted the mattress and laid my pants beneath it to press, and sat down on the chair to read the Bible.

After 20 minutes I closed it in despair. In the meetings, Mr. Johnson was always finding in it exactly what he wanted to know. But though I opened Sister Buffum's book at the beginning, then turned to the middle, then read some near the end, nowhere did it seem to be about my life.

At last I put the Bible on the washstand and got down on my knees beside the bed. The mattress crackled when I leaned my elbows on it and I wished there was a rug on the floor. How did you pray? I wondered. In the meetings, when Mr. Johnson prayed, I just thought his words along with him.

"Heavenly Father," I began, the way he did—and suddenly I forgot about what words I was using. Like a breeze in the room, though the September night was breathless, I felt Him stirring all around me. He was there, so close words were not needed at all. The joy that had begun as I knelt with Sister Buffum at the railing bubbled up to welcome Him. Wave after wave of happiness almost drowned me as I knelt there, telling Him I loved Him, knowing that He loved me.

At last I climbed into the rustling bed and fell asleep. After that, nighttime, which had been so long and dull, was the most thrilling part of every day.

It was probably four or five nights after this first bedside prayer that something different happened. We'd gone door to door all day in Guthrie, a town about 65 miles south of Enid. I closed the door to my small sleeping room, hung my jacket behind it, saw gratefully that there was a rag rug on the floor, and sat down on the chair to pull off my shoes.

I blinked. Those shoes were three feet long! I shook my head, but the optical illusion persisted. Although they were grey with dust, they seemed to glow with a kind of accusing fire, and they were huge—hideous. I tugged them off and shoved them out of sight beneath the bed, but I couldn't get them out of my mind. I held the Bible open on my lap for a few minutes, but as usual found it hard to understand. Then I got down on my knees, but tonight the leaping joy did not come. All I could see were those monstrous shoes and written across them in letters of flame:

STOLEN.

The next day, ringing doorbells in Kingfisher, it continued. Each time I looked at them, the shoes seemed to swell. What could I do? Taking them back was out of the question. After a summer on the roads, the soles were worn, the uppers cracked. It was while I was on my knees beside another bed that the answer came: *Go back and pay for them.*

But . . . I couldn't just walk into Penney's and say, "I stole these shoes." What if they called the police? What if they told my family? My boss?

Yet I couldn't go on walking around in shoes a yard long. Strangely, none of this seemed connected with my new-found companionship with God. I knew stealing was wrong—it was one of the first things my parents taught me. I didn't know a Christian was under a special obligation not to steal. I don't think I even knew that I *was* now a Christian. I only knew that just as it had suddenly become impossible for me to do the idiot brother act, so these shoes would never look right again until they were paid for.

I planned my strategy as carefully as I'd planned the theft.

As soon as we got back to Enid Friday afternoon, I took a walk through the entire department store, studying the clerks, trying to decide which one would be least apt to make a scene about it.

At last I spotted her, a pleasant-looking, heavyset lady behind the counter in Women's Ready-to-Wear. She saw me staring at her and smiled, the edges of her eyes crinkling, and I knew here was a lady who could keep a secret. Best of all, Women's Wear was just to the left of the main doors: I could walk in, give her the money and be back on the sidewalk before anyone else was aware.

At six o'clock we collected our commissions for the week. I counted $3.79 into the right-hand pocket of my suit jacket; not having to wait for change was part of the plan. "Ma'am," I rehearsed my speech once more, "I stole a pair of shoes from your store and now I'm bringing in the money and I will never do it again."

At 6:30 p.m. I was back at Penney's. Good! The saleslady was still on duty. Only . . . she was busy with a customer. I ambled through Men's Wear on the other side of the aisle, waiting for the other woman to leave. But now two more customers arrived.

"Yes, sir? May I help you?"

I started as though the Men's Wear clerk had pointed a gun. "No! I'm—I was just looking!"

I fled into Hats and Gloves, took a long detour through Piece Goods, and returned to Women's Wear. The line at the lady's counter was longer than ever. I had not reckoned on the Friday evening crowds; the very thing that had made the crime possible now made restitution complicated. Feeling more conspicuous than I ever had the evening of the theft, I slunk miserably about the store reading suspicion in every look. By now I would have handed the money to any sales clerk I encountered alone, but all were occupied. I looked up at the mezzanine: lines of people waiting at each desk.

And then I spotted him. A small, grey-haired man sitting at a desk some distance from the others and all by himself. Closing my fist over the bills and coins in my pocket, I plunged through Footwear—feeling the stolen shoes must surely give me away here at the very scene of the crime—and dashed up the stairs.

The plaque on the man's desk read:

MR. ELY

MANAGER

I had selected the head of the entire store.

My prepared speech deserted me. I pulled out the money and dropped it on a corner of his desk. "Sir, I stole a pair of shoes and I'm sorry and here's the money."

I was already heading for the stairs. But the little man was quicker. Gliding on noiseless casters, his chair shot from behind the desk. Without ever rising from his seat Mr. Ely grabbed hold of my arm.

"Not so fast, son! Come here, sit down! I'd like to talk to you."

Not till I crumpled into the chair next to the desk, did the manager release his hold on me. I was free to run for it now, but my legs had turned to water. I pictured the police arriving, all those people on the floor below staring up. . . .

"Tell me, son," the manager asked, "what made you decide to pay for the shoes?"

"You see, Mr. Ely, I had to have shoes for my job. . . ." I stopped. He hadn't asked why I stole them. He asked why I was bringing them back.

"Well, sir, I—" and to my consternation I burst into tears.

"Take your time, son. You've been feeling pretty bad about this, haven't you?"

What could I say—the shoes seemed to swell each time I looked at them? "I went to church and after that I didn't like to wear them."

I heard my own voice with amazement. Till that minute I had not put together those church services and the desire to pay for the shoes.

"I take it," Mr. Ely prodded gently, "that attending church had not been a regular habit?"

And suddenly I found myself telling him the whole story, how I had walked in not knowing what kind of place it was, and how I had gone up front with Sister Buffum. Since I was crying the whole time I thought he wouldn't believe me, but he kept nodding, asking questions.

"And do I understand," he said at last, "that finances continue to present a problem?"

I nodded, feeling my cheeks burn as they always did when I had to confess to poverty.

"And you'll have to give up the door-to-door selling job when school starts?"

When I nodded again, Mr. Ely picked up a telephone on his desk. In a few minutes a young man appeared.

"Mr. Folz," the manager said, "I'd like this young gentleman to have an after-school job in the stock room."

Half an hour later I left Penney's more confused than I'd ever been in my life. I'd gone in to confess to a crime; I emerged on the sidewalk with a new job.

The timing could not have been more fortunate, because now the family had a special need for all our earnings. For two months Mother had had a mystifying illness. "Blood poisoning," the doctors called it, but what caused it, or how to control the boils that covered her body, they did not know. Mr. Stunkle was letting us buy the various medicines they advised on credit; the first time our family had ever run up a debt at a store. And still Mother was no better. The ugly blisters grew larger than ever, the fever so high that some days she did not get out of bed.

This was a terrifying thing for us all, who had never seen Mother so much as sit down to rest. She'd often told us that the only three days she'd ever spent in bed were the days the three of us were born— "and not the whole day then," she'd add.

Dad was working as a night watchman now; when Mother was bad he'd spend the whole day in a chair beside her bed. Bertha Mae would arrive home from her secretarial job to cook and clean and look after the rooms of the Bible students upstairs. "We are interceding for your mother," one of these roomers told me one night, using a word I didn't know. "Would you like to join us?"

After that I often spent the evening upstairs. How those guys could pray, the flow of words never stopping! I had never prayed in front of other people and was far too shy to try, but in my heart I'd echo every one: *Oh yes, Lord Jesus, let it happen just the way he said!*

I could hardly believe they cared so much for a woman they knew only as the person who changed their sheets and dusted their rooms. Till now Mr. Ely was the only one I had told about what had happened in that round-roofed building. Now I told the four students too.

And still there was no change in Mother's condition. Some days she would pull herself painfully out of bed, wincing when her swollen feet touched the floor, to limp to a rear window and survey the sad neglect of her vegetable garden. Others, she did not get even this far, but lay in bed while Dad dipped cloths in the latest concoction from Stunkle's and dabbed her swollen face. Upstairs we redoubled our nightly prayers, and it was there one evening that a new direction opened before me.

As we got up from our knees I blurted out that I wished I could find things in the Bible the way they did. I had given up even trying to follow Lloyd Johnson's instructions; night after night Sister Buffum's gold-edged book lay untouched at my bedside. The students, however, kept opening the Bible, just as Mr. Johnson had, "to see what it says" about whatever we were praying for. And sure enough, there it would be: "Here's what James says to that. . . ."

When I confessed my bewilderment, two of them spoke at once: "Enroll in Bible School!"

It was such a startling idea that I stared back with my mouth open.

"Sure!" another one urged. "You're 18, aren't you?"

Yes. I'd turned 18 two weeks ago. "But. . . ." There were a thousand "buts." Money, for the first thing. If Bertha Mae, valedictorian of her class, had gone to work after high school to help out the family, how could I tell the folks that I—the poorest student of the three—thought I should go to college? Anyhow: "I've still got a year of high school to go," I told them.

But this, it seemed, was no problem. Southwestern Bible College offered high school equivalency courses.

"But. . . enroll for a three-year course?" I groped, trying to get my mind around the idea. Three years more in school, when I'd thought I'd be finished forever in nine months? And what about my after-school job at Penney's?

But the seed was planted. For the first time in my life it began to dawn on me that education could have a purpose. One of our roomers took me around the corner to meet P.C. Nelson, president of the college and a man of such energy and enthusiasm that when I left his office I was all but registered. Most of his students, he assured me, held jobs during the day—classwork was fitted in around working hours.

When my three hours in Penney's stockroom were over next afternoon I went up to the mezzanine to tell Mr. Ely about the new possibility. "So you see, sir, if I transfer to Southwestern I could work here in the mornings too. That is—if you needed me."

"I think we could find you some additional hours," he said. He pointed to the chair beside the desk where I had bawled my eyes out a few weeks before. "Sit down," he said, "and tell me what you plan to do when you get out of Bible college."

When I got out . . . I wasn't even sure I was going in! I had no plan at all, except to find out how people saw all those things in the Bible. But Mr. Ely was reaching into his pocket. He drew out a ten dollar bill: "You'll need books and things. This is just to get you started."

Knowing my parents' distrust of anything "churchy," I approached the subject of Bible school cautiously, sitting at the foot of Mother's bed while Dad lovingly and clumsily patted ointment on her arms. By attending classes at night I pointed out, I'd be able to work twice the hours at Penney's. This was a clinching argument in these days of doctors' and druggist's bills.

And so that fall, 1938, I enrolled in Southwestern Bible College to complete my final year of high school while starting my Bible training. I was not only the youngest student at the school but by far the least prepared. The Old Testament professor would call out a reference and 20 Bibles would open as if by magic to the very place, while I searched the index of Sister Buffum's book for "Habakkuk" or "Second Samuel."

One November morning I arrived in the stockroom in Penney's basement to be told that Mr. Ely wanted to see me upstairs. "Charles," he asked, "how would you like to try your hand at clerking?"

I was placed as a trainee in Men's Wear. Just to walk past the shelves of starched white shirts, the racks of silk ties, filled me with an indescribable sense of well-being. With bewilderment, too, as Mr. Peters, the department head, endeavored to initiate me into the world of gentlemen's apparel. Different outfits for different occasions was a stunning concept, and "color-coordinating" completely beyond me.

Mr. Peters assigned me for several weeks to assist the window dresser as he took down a dummy and put on first a pale blue shirt, then a dark blue suit, a tie that "picks up both blues," and even, to my disbelief, dark blue socks. It was all new and all wonderful, though one of my first discoveries was that my newly-paid-for brown shoes were completely wrong with my Oxford-grey suit. "Black shoes, always, Charles, with grey or black!"

In December with my employee discount I was able to purchase a pair of black shoes. I also bought a plaid jacket with *coordinating* brown trousers, so that I no longer had to wear my suit every day. The trousers were on a two-for-one sale and I chose the second pair for Dad, the longest pant-length they carried. They were to be his Christmas present and I kept picturing his pleasure: at the secondhand store they never had trousers long enough for him. But, Christmas morning, Dad only looked at me in puzzlement.

"But boy, I already have a pair of pants."

It was early one January morning when I was studying at the kitchen table that Bertha Mae came in with Mother's breakfast tray.

"Charles! Mother seems so much better! Look! She finished everything on her plate!"

I put down my book and hurried to Mother's room. She was sitting up in bed, the swelling on her face so much reduced that for the first time in weeks her eyes were fully open. Dad was not yet home from his night watchman job and I sat down in his chair. Mother's arms were still covered with blisters but her hands were nearly their own shape.

"Mother! The man who came here yesterday . . . do you think . . . ?"

She nodded. The day before, while I'd been at work, a man had appeared at the front door and asked permission to pray for her. We never knew his name. Perhaps he was one of the evangelists who frequently stopped at Southwestern where Mother's name, unknown to her, was posted on the prayer list. That Dad had permitted him in the house was a miracle in itself. And now. . . .

By the time I got home from work that afternoon, Mother was enough improved that Dad had moved a chair for her by the window where she could catch the pale winter sunlight.

"Charles, do you know this is the first time I've been able to bear the feel of clothing since last August? Just to have a dress on again!"

I stared from her to Dad. "Has the doctor seen you? What does he say?"

"This has nothing to do with doctors, Charles." Mother's voice dropped almost to a whisper. "When that man . . . when he prayed, Charles, I had this feeling! Like the sunshine, only . . . inside me."

Each day Mother was a little stronger, the blisters fewer. Dad's long frame seemed to come back to life as Mother started busying herself about the house again, shaking dust rags out windows.

When the disfiguring boils had subsided enough "that I won't scare people" Mother announced at supper one night that she intended to go to church the following Sunday. I looked quickly at Dad but though he was staring at her in surprise he voiced no objection. So two days later Mother, Bertha Mae, Bob and I walked around the corner to the Enid Gospel Tabernacle, the church connected with the Bible school. As P. C. Nelson spoke on the coming of Christ in each individual life, I had to keep turning to be sure my family was really there.

Actually, it was one of the few times I attended the Tabernacle. Most Sundays the students at the school were divided into teams for "out-station" work in nearby towns. One of the group would play the guitar while the rest of us sang four-part-harmony gospel songs, then someone would give a short sermon.

I loved it from the first day. One of the members of the team I belonged to was a student from Iowa, Gene Martin, who was to become a lifelong friend. Either Gene or I was generally the one who gave the sermon. To stand up and tell people that Jesus loved them, the way Lloyd Johnson had told me, was the most magnificent thing I could ever do. It didn't matter that our team often outnumbered the congregation. I might be speaking to a couple of farm wives with babies on their laps and one old man whose own snores kept waking him up: I knew that to preach was what I wanted to do the rest of my life.

And yet, side by side with this ambition was another, earlier vision of the future. My private dream world, the world in which I was successful and respected, had never changed from the instant I stepped into the lobby of the Youngblood Hotel (embellished since last July with flourishes from the ballroom of the Allis Hotel in Wichita). What made the two dreams impossible to reconcile was that the preachers I knew had small incomes, old cars, unstylish clothing. Did being a preacher mean giving up the other?

Increasingly I was feeling at home in Penney's Men's Wear. I would catch the eye of the pleasant-faced lady in Women's Ready-to-Wear across the aisle and we would nod, two solid citizens of this solid middle-class world.

Even so, I was not prepared for the morning when Mr. Ely summoned me to his desk on the mezzanine to say that he was recommending me to the company's national organization. As of now I was an employee of the local store only; to be eligible for a permanent position, in line for further promotions, workers had to be approved by a representative of the national headquarters in New York. "Mr. Jenkins will be in Enid next month," Mr. Ely told me, and from then on I lived my days in a fever of determination to make good, my nights in an agony of fear that I would not.

And meanwhile, at home, astonishing changes were taking place. It was strange: I wouldn't have said the others in my family needed to change very much. Mother was the hardest-working, most truthful person I knew. Bertha Mae I don't believe ever had a mean or unkind thought in her life, while Bob, unlike me, was studious and level-headed. As for Dad—he was an utterly upright man who as far as I know never had a sip of liquor and lived only for his wife and family.

And yet, the difference in our home was like night and day. Dad, too had begun accompanying Mother to the services around the corner at Enid Gospel Tabernacle. One by one all four had given their lives to Jesus; now they never missed a service at the small cement-block building next to the Bible school.

Up to this time our family had pretty much kept to ourselves. Now, although our food budget was no larger, there were guests at nearly every meal. Mother toiled as long hours as ever, but now as she scoured and scrubbed she hummed the catchy gospel choruses sung at the Tabernacle. Evenings the house was lively with Bertha Mae's friends from work, Bob's eighth-grade classmates.

But the biggest change was in Dad. As long as I could remember, Dad's outstanding characteristic had been anger—at the electric company, at the economy, at me. Now, incredibly, the anger was gone, leaving in its place a relaxed and joyful person. Not that he got any quieter. His voice still boomed, but the rage and despair was gone. He boomed with the love of life instead of the frustration.

A smaller change caught me by surprise. We were sitting around the living room before I left for classes one night that March, 1939, when Dad drew his pouch of Bull Durham tobacco from his pocket. For a moment he stared at it, almost as though trying to recall what it was. Then his long legs unbent and he pushed himself to his feet. From another pocket came his supply of cigarette papers. "Guess I won't be needing these anymore," he said. He jerked open the door of the pot-bellied stove, tossed papers and tobacco inside, and slammed it shut. It was done in ten seconds; never again did he touch tobacco.

The surprise, to me, was to realize that without ever thinking about it I, too, had stopped smoking. I remembered lighting a cigarette on a lonely street, the night the women came up the stairs at the Oxford Hotel. I saw myself standing in the back of that church, the tobacco pouch in my shirt pocket. That was what—seven months ago? From that night to this I could not recall having a cigarette.

No one had ever told me smoking was wrong, and I doubted anyone had told Dad. Just . . . suddenly and forever, smoking lost its appeal for us both.

One immediate benefit was the money saved. Because in addition to paying off the debt at Stunkle's, I had a new need for cash. I wanted a guitar. Guitars were as important to our services as preaching; if you could get people singing, the rhythm and words did their own persuading. I had even chosen the instrument I wanted: the beautiful maple-top Gibson on page 611 of the Montgomery Ward catalog.

Since the previous May when I'd started traveling for the *Eagle*, Bob had been using my chrome and silver bicycle for his paper route, buying it from me for a dollar a week. Mr. Ely continued to give me an occasional assist with school expenses out of his own pocket. With this help on top of my salary I was able in April to send a money order not only for the guitar but for a plush-lined, imitation-leather case to carry it in.

The same month, Penney's New York representative arrived in Enid. My palms were damp on the railing as I mounted the stairs to the mezzanine. Mr. Jenkins asked me a number of questions in a crisp Eastern voice, drawing me out about my goals and ambitions. I confessed to him my belief that I was to be a preacher. And then, something I had never told anyone else: "But I'll have to have some other job too, Mr. Jenkins, because I want to have—oh, lots of things. Clothes and a car and a house with grass in front."

I felt myself blushing furiously, but I blundered on, putting into words for the first time the dream that had been forming. "I'd have a church of my own you see, Mr. Jenkins, someday. I'd preach there at night, and on Sundays, then during the day work here at Penney's."

In May my guitar was delivered. Now every minute that I was not behind the counter in Men's Wear or attending classes I spent learning the fingering. Late that month there was a message when I arrived for work: Mr. Ely wanted to see me. There on his desk was an envelope with a New York postmark, addressed to me. I had hardly ever received a letter before, let alone from so far.

"Dear Mr. Blair—" was that me? The national office welcomed me as an official member of the Penney's team, wishing me a long and productive career with the store. . . .

The following Monday I stood up in front of the entire staff while Mr. Ely made the announcement. There was applause and handshaking. With the acceptance came a raise, up to the national pay scale, with a second raise due in three months. It was the most triumphant moment of my life, headier even than the penmanship award when I was ten.

The high school graduation ceremony that same week, for those of us at Southwestern who had completed the state requirements, paled beside it. High school already seemed long ago to me, a man with a permanent job and a mission in life.

In July my second raise came through. That month, too, I threw away the clamp I'd been using on the Gibson to form the chords. By continuing to live at home my expenses were at a minimum: in two more years I should graduate from Southwestern an ordained preacher in the Assemblies of God. As far ahead as I could see the future was settled and brighter than I could have dreamed.

Why then was I so restless?

All that summer of 1939 I tried to fight down my dissatisfaction. At home things had never been happier. Gone were Dad's explosions, Mother's worry over money. In fact the poverty in which they'd lived all their lives they now perceived as a Christian virtue.

At work I felt increasingly accepted. The out-station team continued to choose Gene Martin and me as the preachers. To walk away from all this would be madness. Where would I go?

And yet by August I knew that I could not stay any longer in Enid. People were as uncomprehending as I had known they would be. "What could you find somewhere else that you don't have here?"

How could I put into words what was only a twisting beneath my ribs? Sometimes, praying on my knees beside my bed, I would catch little glimpses of the reasons. I kept seeing that milk line at the firehouse: in Enid, no matter how well I might someday do, I would always be the poor-boy-who-made-good. On September 12 I would be 19; I wanted to go where I had nothing to live down. Where I would be just me.

In the college library were magazines carrying advertisements for Bible schools in different parts of the country. I would pore over each one as it arrived. Why I eventually wrote off to North Central Bible School in Minneapolis, Minnesota, I was never sure—except that of all the far-off names, this sounded farthest away of all.

In September came a letter saying that I had been accepted. The next day at Penney's I bought a small suitcase. Of my family, friends and co-workers, only Mr. Ely at the store and Gene Martin at school seemed to understand my need to go.

I didn't have enough clothes to fill the suitcase. My Oxford-grey suit was worn through with constant use; instead I wore the summer-weight beige one I'd bought in the spring. Mother and Dad came with me to the bus station. They both kissed me goodbye, not caring who was watching. The hardest thing I'd ever done was to hold back my tears until the bus had pulled out of sight.

In Wichita I changed to a much larger bus. After dark we pulled into Topeka, Kansas; on a bench in the waiting room I ate the last of the lunch Mother had packed for me. Late that night in Kansas City, Missouri, I bought a hot dog from a counter in the terminal. It cost twice as much as hot dogs in Enid and wasn't half as good.

By breakfast time we were in St. Joseph and I bought coffee and a doughnut. I had completely forgotten about the cost of meals on the trip; I only hoped they would trust me at North Central for part of the tuition. In Des Moines, Iowa, there was an eight-hour wait between buses. I longed to see the city but I was afraid I would never find my way back to the bus station, so I sat on a bench with my suitcase beside me and my guitar on my lap.

It was morning of the third day when we pulled at last into Minneapolis. I gaped out the bus window as the soot-blackened buildings of the downtown loop rose around us. Every few minutes a strange narrow car clanged by, running on tracks like a train, except that there was no engine. Policemen blew their whistles, cars honked until I wanted to jam my fingers in my ears.

I stepped off the bus into the crowded terminal feeling more alone than I ever had in my life. Everyone was in a hurry; everyone but me seemed to know where he was going. Several people cast curious glances at my suit. Everyone here wore dark, somber colors. The pale beige stood out like a neon sign: *Stranger. Doesn't belong.*

I spotted a grilled ticket window and took the letter from North Central out of my pocket. "Sir, could you tell me how to get to 910 Elliott Avenue?"

"Whatsaymac?"

I had to repeat my question twice. He jerked a thumb at an exit sign. "Streetcar, then change to the bus."

Outside the terminal I discovered that it was not only the color of my suit that was wrong: the chill wind went right through the thin summer-weight fabric. In Oklahoma September was a hot dry month; here it was already winter. A streetcar came lurching toward me on its metal rails, far bigger than it had appeared from the bus window. It clanged to a halt and a door in its side slid open. I started up the steps with my suitcase and guitar but was forced back onto the sidewalk by a stream of people getting off.

Now I saw that another door had opened near the front. At the top of the steps was a metal receptacle into which passengers were pushing coins as they entered. But my nickel would not fit; neither would a dime.

The conductor leaned from his glass booth. "Use a token, Mac!"

Having no idea what he was talking about, I poured all the coins in my pocket into his hand. Muttering, he handed most of them back, along with a metal disc that fit into the slot on the box.

It took many questions and several transfers to reach Elliott Avenue. It was more than my light-colored suit that made people stare; my guitar case too was drawing smiles. The guitar, that staple of every Southern worship service, was obviously an oddity in Minneapolis in 1939. I was a green Southern boy in a big Northern city; if I could have found my way back to the depot I would have paid every penny of my tuition money for a return ticket to Enid.

Number 910 was a sprawing five-story brick building. Perhaps the bricks had originally been red; now they were as black as everything else in this city. As I walked up the steps, I imagined faces at the rows and rows of windows: *He brought a guitar! He wore a summer suit!*

The huge lobby was filled with groups of chattering students. Everybody seemed to know everybody else.

"Hi! I'm Tim Hollingsworth. What's your name?"

I looked up into the face of a tall blond young man with a friendly grin.

"Charles," I managed to get out.

"Great to meet you, Charles! You just arriving?"

At the sound of the first friendly voice I'd heard in three days, the tears I'd been keeping in check rose dangerously near the surface.

"Tell you what, Charles, we'll go into Mrs. Ketter's office right here and find out what room they've got you in."

Tim did all the talking as Mrs. Ketter looked up my room assignment, locker number and meal hours. I was stunned to learn that students were expected to pay for their monthly meal tickets in advance. The cost of the first month's meals, along with my expenses en route, meant that in the next office I was unable to produce the required full tuition for the first semester. Again Tim came to the rescue, assuring the registrar that by midterm I'd have the remainder. I did actually have in my pocket a letter from Mr. Ely to the manager of the Penney's in Minneapolis, but I could not trust my voice to tell Tim this.

Tim kept up a cheerful commentary as he steered me through the lobby to the elevators. I was grateful that I had ridden the one at the Youngblood and knew enough to turn and face the door as we rode up to the fourth floor. Room 428 contained four beds, four small study desks and a communal closet along one wall. Although no one was there, it was obvious from the clothes stewn about that my three roommates had already arrived. The bed nearest the door was the only one unclaimed; Tim helped me make it up with the sheets and blankets folded at the foot. "You can put that under the bed," he said with a noncommittal glance at my guitar, and gratefully I shoved it out of sight.

And so began the most stretching time of my life. Because of the year at Southwestern I entered North Central as a second year student. But the real education took place outside of school. The first Sunday I went with some other students to the enormous Minneapolis Gospel Tabernacle. Here among these sober Swedes and Norwegians there was no handclapping, no cries of *Amen!* When the choir filed in wearing long robes, I could hardly suppress a gasp. Weren't choir robes the very embodiment of "external show"? But no thunderbolt fell from heaven and I felt a window opening into the narrow room I had labeled "the only right way" to worship.

More surprises were to follow. One day Tim Hollingsworth said "I've got an extra ticket to the symphony, Saturday. Care to come?"

I would have died rather than admit I did not know what "the symphony" was and I said yes. That afternoon, however, traveling to my part-time job at Penney's, I saw a poster advertising Saturday night's symphony *concert,* and could almost feel the flames of hell. At Southwestern I had learned that there were only two kinds of music: gospel music and sin music. I had never heard of Beethoven, Schumann and other names on the poster but the titles of their compositions did not sound like anything you would play on a guitar.

Saturday night four of us drove in Tim's car across the bridge into St. Paul. At night the grey dinginess of the streets disappeared and the Twin Cities sparkled with light. The only concerts I had ever heard were at the bandshell in Enid; I had never imagined so many instruments as I saw on the stage of that auditorium.

Then the conductor raised his baton and heaven opened. Down poured sounds such as I had never known existed. Soaring, glorious sounds that made me want to weep and laugh both at once. Whether it was church music I did not know, but that it was God's music I was sure.

Money, however, continued a problem. Right away I had to buy an overcoat, the first one I'd ever needed. Laundry was another expense I hadn't reckoned on: shirts and underwear I could do myself, but sheets had to go out, and in smoky Minneapolis it seemed my light beige suit was always at the cleaners. Then winter began in earnest: for the first time in my life I needed gloves, overshoes, a scarf.

In December I met the man who was to affect everything that happened afterwards. He was the Reverend A.M. Alber, a huge, white-haired bear of a man, as tall as my father and a third again his weight, who was Superintendent of the Assemblies of God churches for the Nebraska District. Two of my roommates, Carlyle Beebe and Paul Wagner, were from Nebraska and Reverend Alber stopped by our room whenever he came to lecture at the school. He would ease his giant frame onto one of our small desk chairs, his shock of hair gleaming like a Minnesota snowfall in the light of the study lamp, and encourage us to hold fast to our dreams.

As the long winter gave way to a breathcatching Northern spring, I became part of a team serving country churches, as at Southwestern. I preached in a gentler, less passionate manner now, modeling myself after Dr. Linquist at the Minneapolis Gospel Tabernacle. But I was still a raw, untrained speaker who knew little about the Bible and less about the world.

How then could I explain what happened each time I stood up to deliver one of these stumbling sermons? The small congregation would be made up of hard-muscled no-nonsense people whose grandparents had cleared these Northern forests and to whom an inexperienced 19-year-old boy had nothing, in a natural way, to teach. But as I opened my mouth to speak, something bigger, stronger, better than myself took over. I forgot where I was and who I was, forgot everything except the incredible love of God for each person in that place. And these farmers and woodsmen and shopkeepers wept, and called out Jesus' name, and came forward to give Him their lives. I knew it wasn't my words, and yet I also knew that I was somehow meant to be doing what I was doing.

How then was I to get the necessary ordination? The cost of living in Minneapolis was simply too high for me. At the beginning of May the last month's meal ticket had to be purchased. May 1 arrived and I didn't have the money. With a heart as heavy as the day I first entered the lobby, I went to Mrs. Ketter's office to tell her I would not be able to complete even this year at North Central.

I had a standing offer of a full-time job at the Minneapolis Penney's. What other choice was there? Mother's last letter had had great news: Dad had found work again as a lineman. But that meant they'd be moving again from town to town, giving up the house in Enid. Here in Minneapolis I could stay with a student who lived in town and work at Penney's until I had saved enough to go back to school.

Packing my suitcase was easy, saying goodbye to friends like Tim Hollingsworth, Carlyle Beebe, and Paul Wagner was not. We sat about the room, my last night in the dorm, making elaborate plans for reunions that each of us knew in his heart would never be held. I looked up to see Reverend Alber's large bulk filling the doorway. "What's this they tell me downstairs? You're leaving North Central, Charles?"

I explained about the meal ticket. He knew I'd been living from one financial crisis to the next.

"How do you feel about it?" he asked. "Leaving school to go to work?"

"It should be okay," I said with what I trusted was nonchalance. "I mean, I like the store and—" The treacherous tears that all my life had betrayed my feelings pricked the back of my eyes.

The other students looked away, feeling my embarrassment, but Reverend Alber continued to stare at me, a curious, scrutinizing gaze. "What do you want to do, more than anything on earth?" he asked.

"To preach," I said instantly, not even stopping to think.

Still he continued to study me. "If you want to preach," he said at last, "I can find a platform for you right now in Nebraska. I'm setting up the District summer program and I could use a youth speaker."

It was as though the sun had burst through an overcast sky. The Assemblies of God at that time required only the "equivalent" of three years Bible training before a candidate could be considered for ordination. The experience I would gain as a preacher to youth groups, besides being the thing I longed to do, would mean I was still moving toward my goal of one day becoming a minister.

At the end of the week I drove with Reverend Alber to Burton, Nebraska, then to other camp meetings around the state. At these summer gatherings ministers from nearby towns would be present. Some would invite me back to speak to the young people of their home churches that fall, and in this way I gradually established a year-round itinerant ministry.

My favorite times were car trips with Reverend Alber. On these long drives across the sand hills of Nebraska he shaped my career, as he did for scores of young men before and since. Don't speak in abstractions, he'd tell me. Talk about things you really know. Don't spend money on dating; there'll be time to meet girls and find a wife later. Use every penny you can save to do two things. Travel to increase your knowledge of the world. And buy books. Every week read at least one book from cover to cover.

For the next two years I followed his advice scrupulously. Next to the hours on my knees beside my bed each night, the time I spent reading now became my favorite part of the day. Usually I would be housed with the pastor of the church where I was holding youth meetings. I would ask permission to browse through his library, spending blissful mornings feeling my narrow horizons expand.

I also haunted secondhand bookstores, using my share of the "love offerings" collected at each service to start a library of my own. As I read I would look up words I did not know in the dictionary, then work them into my talks. In the households where I stayed there was no place to practice my sermons. So I would go out in the fields, stand on a rise of ground, and inform a startled herd of cattle that *supercilious* attitudes could only lead to *unprecedented* problems.

Through 1940 and 1941 I traveled the length and breadth of Nebraska, learning from the pastors, living with their bighearted families. I remember that I was reading a collection of sermons in Bayard, in the extreme west of the state, one Sunday afternoon in early December, 1941, when the pastor burst into the study.

"Charles, we're at war!"

I ran with him to the kitchen where his wife and Bob Teague, the handsome dark-haired young pianist who now traveled with me, were bent over a round-topped Crosley radio. For a long time we listened to the bewildering news. Where was Pearl Harbor? Why would the Japanese bomb it?

Since I had turned 21 in September I had to go home at once to register for the draft. I hitched a number of rides down to Cherokee, Oklahoma, where my parents were currently living. In Cherokee they had found a tiny, pastorless church into which they poured all the passion of their new faith. After a long day climbing poles and stringing wires, Dad did repairs on the neglected building and gave it the fresh coat of paint he would never have squandered on the place he lived in, while Mother delivered the Sunday messages that drew a growing congregation. They took no money for this work; indeed I suspected that much of Dad's paycheck went into that little church.

It was April before I heard from the draft board. I'd applied for the Chaplaincy Corps and I tore open the official government envelope eagerly. My application had been denied. Instead, since I had listed my occupation as "youth evangelist" I'd been classified 4-F—exempt from service. Bob had received the same classification two weeks earlier. I returned to Cherokee to try this time to enlist as a Chaplain's assistant but was again turned down.

In May the Assemblies of God held their annual statewide

meeting to elect officers. When I arrived Reverend Alber took me aside.

"Charles," he said, "I've put your name up for state president of Christ's Ambassadors." This was the young people's organization.

"But I'm not ordained." The president had to be a duly certified Assemblies of God minister.

"You're scheduled to be examined by the state elders this afternoon," he went on. He felt confident, he said, that my experience speaking throughout the state these past two years, plus the study I was doing on my own, would convince the elders that I was qualified for ordination.

I did not share his optimism and my legs would scarcely carry me into the church building in Grand Island, on the banks of the Platte, where the 1942 convention was being held. For two hours the state officers questioned me about my schooling, my beliefs, my commitment to Christ. Apparently they were satisfied, because the following day when Reverend Vogler from the national headquarters in Springfield, Missouri, arrived in Grand Island, I was sitting at the front of the church with eight other young men awaiting ordination.

Mr. Vogler preached a sermon emphasizing the life-committing step we were about to take. Then one by one we stepped forward to kneel at the railing. Mr. Vogler for the national church and Mr. Alber for Nebraska District stepped down from the platform to lay their hands on our heads. The words in Reverend Alber's rich bass were brief:

"Charles Blair, we now ordain you into the full-time ministry of the Lord."

But for me they were the marching orders that would govern the rest of my life. The knowledge that I, the most unlikely person on earth, had been set aside to serve God with all my strength, was so overwhelming that when next day, as Reverend Alber had predicted, I was elected state president of Christ's Ambassadors, I was scarcely aware of the proceedings.

It was the start of the busiest year I'd ever spent. As president I was expected to visit every one of the scores of local youth groups across the state, and in addition represent Nebraska around the country. The war, however, made any kind of travel difficult. Train and bus seats, when they could be had, needed to be booked weeks ahead. I had known how to drive ever since the out-station work at Southwestern, and occasionally I would borrow a car to get a meeting. This also meant, though, using the other person's precious gas coupons.

"Why don't you get a car of your own?" Reverend Alber asked me one day in July. "Ministers get an extra gas ration, you know."

A car of my own! In my daydreams this was no trustworthy old second hand Model-A, but a sleek new sports model. It was only a dream though—until that conversation with Reverend Alber. If I was to do my job and not be a constant drain on other people's gas allotment, why, I'd have to have a car! As for that sensible Model-A, to my secret delight I found that secondhand cars just weren't available. Anyone with any kind of car in 1942 was hanging on to it. I went before the ration board in Lincoln, Nebraska, where I stayed between trips with a family named Throne, and applied for a new-car permit.

It came through almost at once. With the government form in my hand I almost ran to the automobile showroom. And there stood my car in the window: a Chevrolet "fastback" built like a torpedo, the rear end swooping to a streamlined point. It was bright red.

I knew I should talk over such a major purchase with all kinds of people, especially Reverend Alber who was putting up the down payment. But I had no more ability to resist that car than a moth can resist a floodlight, and from then on Bob Teague and I traveled in style.

Army bases had sprung up around the state and now that we had transportation we volunteered our services to the chaplains. The men seemed to enjoy the meetings we held, but I was painfully aware that a lot of these guys were going to be killed somewhere overseas while I was driving around Nebraska in a flashy red car.

Men our age in civilian clothes, in fact, had become rarities. It took Bob and me a while to perceive one result. All we knew was that by July there had stopped being an extra bedroom in any pastor's home in Nebraska. Wherever we went, the parsonage was being repainted or a great aunt had just arrived from Montana. Instead, we'd be placed with "one of our finest families." They were fine folks, indeed, kind, hospitable, feasting us with enormous meals that included a month's ration of butter, meat and sugar.

It was August before it dawned on us how very many unmarried girls lived in these households. Bob and I were terror-struck. With the car payments and gasoline, plus the books I was buying, I didn't have enough to take a girl for an ice cream soda, let alone get serious. Besides, the daughters of the "finest families" were such pale, solemn young women. Following Reverend Alber's advice, I had not so much as spoken with a girl, outside a group, for more than two years. That didn't stop me from thinking about them. My fantasy girl, in addition to being a Christian, was brilliant and beautiful, with the wardrobe of a fashion model and the figure of a movie star.

Toward the end of August Bob and I drove out to Lexington, Nebraska, near the center of the state, where a week-long camp meeting was to climax the summer season. The campground was several miles out of town in a field beside some train tracks, and Bob and I gratefully set up a sleeping tent, far from the ministrations of the finest families. Our first job, as often, was to help erect the meeting place. Lexington was located on the main line of the Burlington Railroad; every quarter hour, it seemed, a train would thunder past. As I sawed planks for benches I wondered how we'd ever make ourselves heard during the meetings.

After the first day we simply stopped trying. All singing and preaching would halt while the train lumbered by, 200, 250 freight cars at a time in that flat country, while black smoke poured through the open sides of our temporary building. Still it was the best meeting of the summer, with hundreds of families camping in tents across the fields. Thursday was Christ's Ambassadors Day, with representatives of local chapters from all over the state attending. I gave the evening address and afterwards stood outside greeting people. It was the night of the August full moon, the train tracks glowed silver.

And it was then I saw her, standing in the cluster of people waiting to shake hands, the moon making a halo of her light brown hair. She was maybe five-foot-three with a trim, athletic figure and a pixie face set off with a touch of lipstick. I could not see the color of her eyes in the moonlight; I only knew she was the most beautiful girl I had ever seen.

The most out of reach too. Everything about her—her clothes, her hair, some indefinable air of self-assurance—spoke of privilege and wealth, and I gazed at her with the same kind of awe I felt for the moon itself. After an age we were face to face. And at that moment a freight train thundered abreast of us.

"What's your name?" I shrieked through the din.

But a cloud of coal smoke enveloped us and when it cleared away she had moved on. When the long handshaking was over, I found her in a chattering group. "I didn't get your name, miss?"

She turned around, "Betty," she said. "Betty Ruppert."

"And ah—" What else could I ask? "You're here as a representative?"

Bob Teague strolled up and I had to introduce him, acutely aware of his dark good looks. Betty was president of the Christ's Ambassadors chapter in McCook, Nebraska, she told us.

McCook! I thought gleefully. In the south of the state, almost at the Kansas border, it was one of the towns I had not yet been to in my program of visiting each chapter in the state.

"We were just planning to come to McCook! Next week in fact!"

"But," Betty looked startled, "we meet the third Thursday, Mr. Blair. We won't be meeting again till September 20."

"That's what I meant, of course. We were planning to come September 20."

Bob was staring at me. For weeks he'd been planning a trip home once the summer camp-meeting season was over.

"Uh . . . unfortunately, Bob can't come," I fumbled, quite content to make this particular visit unaccompanied.

"I'll tell Pastor and Mrs. Smitley," Betty said, "so they can have a room ready for you."

A room at the parsonage? Where were the painters and plumbers and visiting aunts now that I needed them?

Betty held out her hand: "The group will be so pleased to know you're coming." Then she was gone and the moon seemed to go under a cloud. The group will be pleased? Won't *you* be pleased, Betty? Not even a little?

The next three weeks seemed like three months. When Bob took off to see his folks, I drove straight south, arriving at the startled Smitleys' two days early. Pastor Smitley was a cordial, energetic man, full of statistics about the price local farmers were getting for sugar beets, but he volunteered nothing about Betty.

Mrs. Smitley was more satisfactory. "A marvelous girl! I don't know what we'd do without Betty—and when you think what that family's been through! Of course her mother's a wonderful person too, and so is her sister. Patty's only 15 but she's teaching Sunday School this fall too."

I was longing to ask what the family had "been through" but Mrs. Smitley's reflections were not easy to stop. Listening, I learned that Betty was 19, that in addition to teaching Sunday school and leading the youth group, she was the church pianist, and that during the day she had a civil service job at the local ration board. "She was offered a marvelous job in Washington, away back East. But she didn't feel she should leave her mother and Patty. More coffee, Mr. Blair? And clever with a needle! Of course, she gets that from her mother."

Mrs. Smitley had a great deal to say about the talents of Mrs. Ruppert and the two Ruppert girls; she never mentioned a Mr. Ruppert. And then suddenly the coffee in my cup turned to acid.

"Yes," Mrs. Smitley was saying, "Hal Winner's getting a marvelous girl. Betty will be such an asset to him on that big farm, though of course we'll hate to lose her here. But that won't be for a couple of years anyhow, not till he's out of the service."

"A couple of years till they—get married, you mean?" I managed to ask.

"Yes, and I'm not sure it's wise to wait. What do you think? Everyone's known all along that Hal and Betty would get married one day. His aunt and uncle are such marvelous people!" There followed a glowing description of a Mr. and Mrs. Anderson who—in some way not clear to me—had "come to the rescue" of the Rupperts years before. Hal Winner, their nephew, had grown up on a farm in western Nebraska, but came here to stay with the Andersons while he attended McCook Junior College. And been handed the most beautiful girl in the world on a silver platter, I raged inwardly, just because the Rupperts were grateful to his aunt and uncle.

Because I'd arrived early I attended the Wednesday midweek prayer service, standing with Pastor Smitley in the door of the church to meet people as they arrived. There was Betty, coming up the walk with a stylishly dressed woman, and a pretty girl of 15. I saw at once where Betty got her slender good looks; Mrs. Ruppert was a stunning woman, brunette like Betty, while Patty's hair was cornsilk-yellow.

They all shook hands with Pastor Smitley, and then Betty held out her hand to me. But I was staring at her other one, the one with the diamond ring that I had not seen in the moonlight by the train tracks. "Good evening, Mr. Blair. I'd like you to meet my mother, Mrs. Ruppert, and my sister Patty."

I don't want to meet anybody, I wanted to shout, before I know if you love Hal Winner, or if you're just marrying him because everybody always said that you would!

Pastor Smitley had me sit beside him on the platform, where it was all I could do to keep my eyes off Betty at the piano. She played wonderfully. Not like some church pianists who got by with a few standard chords, but like a musician. Try as I might to keep my mind on Pastor Smitley's sermon, I found it drifting to Betty and me, married, traveling together as a husband-wife team! To stick a girl like her out on some farm at the end of nowhere—what would she do, play the piano for the pigs?

We were singing the closing hymn when my strategy occurred to me. She would be playing for the Christ's Ambassadors meeting tomorrow. What could be more natural than to ask her to stay after the service tonight and run through the music? A couple of questions—casual, seemingly disinterested—and I'd be able to tell, I knew I would, how she really felt about Hal Winner.

"Of course I'll be glad to stay," she said when I asked. "Mother and Patty won't mind waiting."

"Well, I—it's no trouble at all to drive you home, Miss Ruppert, if they want to go on."

"Oh no." The idea seemed to startle her. "We always go

home together."

And so we rehearsed the next night's program with Patty and Mrs. Ruppert looking on. When the four of us left the church at last I was surprised to see only my own car in the parking lot.

"You live close by," I surmised.

"Just a mile-and-a-half," Mrs. Ruppert said.

"Let me drive you home," I said—they must have used up their gas ration this month.

It was too dark to see the Rupperts' house, except that it appeared smaller than I expected. The lawn, I saw in the car headlights, was freshly raked and seeded with new grass. I switched off the motor and turned to Mrs. Ruppert.

"Tomorrow night, M'am, after the meeting, may I have permission to drive Betty home?"

"Why, I guess so, if Betty wants to," Mrs. Ruppert said.

And so the next night, when the last of the youth group had said goodnight, I walked Betty out to the parking lot. Good! Again my car was the only one in sight.

"I'm glad you didn't bring your car tonight, Betty. That must mean that you won't mind too terribly driving home with me?"

"Bring my car?" she laughed. "Heavens, we don't have a car!"

I puzzled over this extraordinary piece of information as we drove. Too soon, we reached her house. "Could you . . . sit here and talk a minute?" I asked.

"Of course. Just let me tell Mother we're here."

She ran up the front walk, lithe and graceful in the headlights, while I racked my brain for some impressive topic. Outreach to the local community! That was it! I remembered a lecture I'd heard on that at North Central.

But when Betty climbed into the front seat beside me what I heard myself say instead was, "Betty, what does a person do when he's had an ideal in his mind for years, and when he meets her she's already spoken for?"

In the awful silence that followed I knew I'd blown my single chance—if in fact I'd ever had one. "It's, ah, kind of late to be planting grass, isn't it?" I blundered on. "Or maybe September's the best time. Instead of spring."

"Grass?" Betty said, finding her voice at last. "Oh, you mean the front yard!" She gave the rippling laugh I loved. "I'll tell you a secret about that grass, Mr. Blair. There's none planted and there's none going to be."

"But . . . it's raked and ready."

"I keep it raked just because it looks neater. But at first . . ." her voice dropped as though she were making a shameful confession. "At first, Mr. Blair, I was so terribly, terribly ashamed of being poor that I'd go out and rake it, hoping the people who walked by would think what you thought—that we'd just planted some, or were just going to."

Poor? This radiant girl? The Rupperts were poor . . . like the Blairs?

She was chuckling at the memory. "I was only 11, of course. Children are so self-conscious, aren't they, about what people think!"

Children are self-conscious . . . and so are grownups, Betty! So am I! But you're not. If you were ever poor, you discovered some secret that kept you from *feeling* poor. . . .

Far into the night, in my room at the Smitleys', I lay awake recalling the rest of our conversation and the wrenching story Betty had told:

Until she was 11, Betty had lived the contented life of any small-town Nebraska child, with dolls and piano lessons and Sunday afternoon outings in the family car. Her father was the linotype operator on the McCook *Daily Gazette*. He was blond and good-looking—it was from him that Patty got her corn-yellow hair—fun to be with and popular with the other men at the paper. Betty adored him. He was the pitcher on the local softball team and when Betty was nine he bought her her own mitt and taught her to throw.

Because his drinking went on mainly at night, Betty for a long time remained unaware of it. She remembered only the final terrible months when he became violent with her mother and seven-year-old Patty, although never with her. The crisis came when Mrs. Ruppert sought the help of a local minister. Betty's father was enraged. God was the invention of those too weak to stand on their own two feet. In a drunken haze one night he concluded that the clergyman and his wife must be having an affair. He loaded his shotgun, telephoned the minister and invited him to the house "to pray." The man never appeared, although Mr. Ruppert waited all night by the door with the loaded gun.

Shortly after that, Betty returned from a school chorus rehearsal one late afternoon to find her father striking her little sister. "I'll slap the religion out of you!" he roared. "I'll teach you to sneak off to church!"

Betty's diminutive mother was trying to drag the furious man away from the little girl. Betty joined her and together they pulled the two apart. As Betty and Patty ran from the house they could hear their father turn his rage on their mother. They fled to the house next door where their neighbor telephoned the police.

As they waited, sobbing, at the neighbor's window, they saw the front door of their own house open and their mother stumble down the steps, their father behind her. At that moment the patrol car arrived; it took both policemen to get Virgil Ruppert into the car.

Betty had not seen him again since that afternoon, although she had written him whenever she had an address, and received an occasional letter in reply.

"He sent me this watch two years ago when I graduated from high school." In the dark front seat she had held up a tiny luminous dial.

From the divorce proceedings, instituted by him, they had learned that he was working as a linotype operator in Nevada, later that he had remarried and moved to Oregon. Not a penny ever came to the family in McCook. His first wife believed in God: then let God support her.

And so God had, although, Betty admitted, at a rather different level. For seven dollars a month, her mother found a furnished room with a bathroom down the hall shared with other roomers on the floor. For two years the three of them shared the room's single bed, sleeping crosswise on the lumpy mattress and cooking their meals on a hot plate in the corner. "We ate a lot of potato soup."

Her mother supported them by taking in sewing, while Betty took housework jobs on Saturdays—washing, ironing, scrubbing floors for 25¢ a day. In addition to their own expenses, Mrs. Ruppert learned that her husband had run up debts at local stores. The largest was a bill for $90 at the Deluxe Grocery. Mrs. Ruppert called on the grocer and promised to pay it back, 50¢ a week. Five years later she told the girls with pride that every one of their father's debts was paid.

Meanwhile the church became both home and family. Often they would find a sack of groceries in the hallway outside their room, never with a name, only "God loves you" on a bit of folded paper. Church friends provided shoes, doctors' fees, school supplies—all too frequently I heard the name "Anderson."

When Betty turned 13 she began charging 50¢ a day for housework. By then her mother had started doing alterations for a men's clothing store and with this increased income they were able to rent the house in front of which we had parked.

Without money for lessons there seemed no way for Betty to continue her music. Then she learned that the high school orchestra lacked a bassoon player; the school offered both instrument and instruction. "But it was such a big, long, clumsy thing!" Every day she lugged the heavy case the mile-and-a-half to school, then a mile-and-a-half the other direction to church where an orchestra was also forming. "When it snowed I used to cry, my fingers got so cold."

By now I'd experienced two Nebraska winters myself. I pictured a small determined girl leaning into the wind, tears freezing on her cheeks. But there'd been no trace of self-pity in her reminiscences. "God was looking out for us, just as Mother said. Lugging a bassoon develops even better muscles than baseball. And trying to make a sound come out of it! The school doctor used to say I had the best lungs in McCook."

She had looked down at her glowing wristwatch. "It's after eleven. I have to be at the ration board early!" She jumped from the car before I could move. "Thank you for speaking to our group tonight, Mr. Blair," she called from the walk. "And for letting me ramble on about myself this way!"

The door of the house had closed behind her. Thank you for letting me talk about myself . . . was that a brief, small hint of encouragement?

It was amazing how effortlessly my schedule opened up, the rest of that week. "Too bad you can't be here Sunday for our regular service," Pastor Smitley said unsuspectingly at breakfast next morning.

"Oh I can!" I said, and made a hurried phone call to Bob Teague. Bob was to lead the music in his hometown church next Sunday and I'd planned to join him there. But by now I knew that I was never again going to meet anyone like Betty Ruppert. Betty had been as poverty-stricken as I. More so. My family may have needed government milk; hers had depended on charity for food, clothing, everything. She'd hated being poor too, just as I had. The bare yard raked as if for grass seed showed that. But she hadn't hated herself because of it—there was the difference. She hadn't needed to pretend, as I had, that she was something or somebody else.

For the next two days I hung around the Ruppert house. Betty was at work and Patty in school but Mrs. Ruppert seemed to welcome having someone to talk to as she sat at the dining room table letting out the seams on a man's suit jacket. She needed no prompting to speak about her girls and told me much that Betty had left out. Knowing that there would be no chance of going on to college, Betty had taken advantage of everything McCook High School had to offer. Everything free, Mrs. Ruppert corrected herself. She'd joined the pep club, but dropped out when she learned that members had to buy uniforms. And the activities card which let students into school sports events cost three dollars and so was out of the question. But the other after-school programs—the drama club, the Latin club, the honor society—she took part in everything. She had graduated in the top tenth of her class with the longest list of extracurricular activities of anyone in school and almost a full year's extra academic credits.

"And all this time she cleaned for people, besides all the church things she did."

Saturday Mrs. Ruppert invited me to stay for dinner. "I'm so glad you're staying for the service tomorrow," Betty said as I dug into the fricasseed chicken.

"I'm glad I could stay too," I said, hoping she did not see the flush of pleasure I could feel creeping up my neck.

"Hal will be there," Betty went on, "and I just know the two of you will enjoy each other."

The chicken was a stone in my mouth. Enjoy him? She had a strange idea of enjoyment, that was all. I managed to get the lump down my throat. "Hal?" I croaked.

"Yes. He's a Marine pilot, you know. Stationed in Omaha right now, but the Andersons expect him tonight. I can't wait for you to meet him."

I could wait. I could wait till the end of time. "I ah . . . I hope Bob Teague will be all right tomorrow," I said. "Handling the meeting in Bayard alone. Kind of a tough assignment—town where he grew up and everything."

Extremely tough. In fact I didn't see how I could desert old Bob at a time like this. It was my duty to be in Bayard. I left the Rupperts' early, made my excuses to the Smitleys and before anyone was awake next morning was speeding in my Chevrolet fastback away from McCook.

I spent the rest of the fall circling miserably about Betty's town, accepting any preaching invitation that would take me within dropping-in distance. As Nebraska's representative I had a number of speaking dates in more distant places—Detroit, Denver, Phoenix. But like a needle in a compass I would swing back always toward McCook.

"I misjudged you, Charles," Reverend Alber confessed as we drove to a youth retreat in Pallisades, Nebraska (McCook,

35 miles). "I'd have said you'd gravitate to the glamour assignments—big crowds, that sort of thing. But no group is too small for you to get excited about. I like that."

I reddened under the undeserved praise. But how could I tell him that I was pursuing a fantasy? In December all the Rupperts could talk about was the week's leave Hal was getting at Christmas. "His parents are coming in from the farm," Mrs. Ruppert said as her fingers guided a trouser leg beneath the hammering needle of her sewing machine. "They'll stay with the Andersons but Hal's going to stay here."

Driving to Oklahoma to be with my own family, I tried to block out the image of Betty and Hal together. My parents had left Cherokee and were living in another small town while Dad worked on lines in the vicinity. The war meant a shortage of skilled electrical workers—long hours and high pay—but they were renting as simple a house as ever. They came out to the dirt road to greet me.

"Kind of a fancy car for a preacher, isn't it, son?" Dad worried.

When she saw how many Christmas presents I had brought, Mother joined in: "Charles, we have Jesus now! We don't need all these things!"

But you never did! I wanted to say. When did you ever want things for yourselves?

I thought about it again that night, lying beside Bob in a couch-turned-bed in the living room. Weren't all of us finding in religion reasons for doing exactly what we'd always done? In the folks' case doing without; in mine, the desire to succeed, to travel, to make a name for myself.

It was a good Christmas, though, because Dad and Mother were so singingly happy. As I suspected, they were spending most of Dad's paycheck to paint and repair yet another rural church which had fallen on hard times. Bertha Mae did not get home; she was traveling with an evangelistic team. Bob, now in his final year of high school, had also decided on the ministry.

In January I fought snow drifts across the highway to visit

McCook. "Did you have a nice holiday?" Mrs. Ruppert asked as we waited for Betty to come downstairs.

"Fine, thank you. How was yours?" I forced myself to ask.

"Very nice. Only—I know it wasn't easy for Betty and Hal."

At that moment Betty appeared in the doorway, her light brown hair swinging about her shoulders. I'd warned myself during these weeks apart that I'd exaggerated her beauty. But in her red sweater she was lovelier than I remembered. As always my glance traveled from her blue-green eyes to the third finger of her left hand.

There was no ring.

"Betty! It's a beautiful day for a drive!"

Mother and daughter looked dubiously at the sleet pinging against the window. But without a word Betty put on her coat.

Two blocks away I pulled as far to the side of the road as the drifts would allow. "You and Hal . . . " I began.

Betty looked down at her lap. "I guess it was the hardest thing I've ever done," she said. "He's been so kind to me. All of them have. But I began to realize we didn't know each other well enough to make a decision like this."

I had to raise my voice over the thudding of my heart. "Betty, the day I saw you I knew you well enough! Well enough to know there couldn't be anyone else for me. Oh Betty, will you marry me?"

"Yes, Charles. I've already told Hal. He . . . he wished us well. From his heart."

Why had I ever disliked Hal? Hal was a great guy! The Andersons were great, and McCook was great. In fact the whole world was a wide wonderful place where miracles still happened.

We decided to be married in May, at the close of my year as state president. "Sunday the ninth!" Betty said. "That's Mother's Day. Somehow that seems right when Mother's the one who kept our family together."

The next few months Bob and I crowded in as many meetings in as many states as we could. With his looks and musical talent Bob was constantly receiving job offers for when our year of youth work was over. For me it was harder, partly because I wasn't sure what kind of work to turn to. Should Betty and I be looking for a church to pastor, or should we travel, at least at first, as a husband-wife evangelistic team? We inclined toward the latter. Betty was as eager to see the country as I was, and we were too young for most churches to consider as pastors anyhow. I was 22, Betty wouldn't turn 20 until two days before our wedding.

I gave a lot of thought to our honeymoon too. Of the places I'd been, the city of Denver excited me most. Betty had been there too, with her school band. Raised on the prairies, both of us responded to that high, bold city with its backdrop of snow-topped mountains.

Keeping it a surprise from Betty, I wrote the minister of the little Assemblies of God church in downtown Denver where I'd held some youth services, asking him to reserve a room for us for four nights "in some really first-class hotel." It must have strained his sense of frugality, for Central Assembly was a struggling new congregation meeting in a building designed as a movie theater, but he wrote back that in accordance with my wishes he'd booked us into the Brown Palace.

But finances, I'd discovered the past couple of years, were simply no problem. In wartime America everybody seemed to have money, and not enough consumer goods to spend it on. The offerings at Bob's and my meetings were larger than either of us could believe; I was now giving away, as my own offering, more than I'd made in my best week as a magazine salesman. Now that my engagement was known there were household donations too: bedding and dishes, silverware and table lamps, until my bedroom at the Thrones' resembled a department store annex.

Since all my dreams were coming true, I decided to be choosey about the weather this coming summer too. We were honeymooning in Denver; what was to prevent us setting up our summer meetings in the mountains! For once, no sweltering in a dusty tent in 110° heat. The mountains beyond Denver were filled with bustling summer colonies who certainly needed the gospel as badly as the ranchers on the plains. Zealously I wrote every resort-town church I could get the name of, and got enthusiastic acceptances. They were a bit inaccessible, they cautioned, but I wrote back that I had a car and a C-card.

Because of the wartime travel situation neither my family nor old friends like Gene Martin could make it to McCook for the wedding. I was doubly grateful, therefore, that Reverend Alber had swallowed his disapproval of such an "early" marriage, and agreed to perform the ceremony along with Pastor Smitley. The wedding was set for three o'clock Sunday afternoon, May 9.

"Be sure you're here for the rehearsal Saturday afternoon," Betty reminded me over the phone. In Lincoln Saturday morning I hung my new black pin-stripe wedding suit in the back seat for the 250-mile drive. Then with Bob Teague, who was best man, I lugged out armloads of wedding gifts. It took us half a dozen trips, till the trunk of the Chevy was full and the back seat packed to the roof. There was a round of embraces from the Thrones and it was nearly ten o'clock when we pulled away from the curb.

I'd driven perhaps 20 blocks when it happened.

I never even saw the car that hit us. It shot out of a side street, ignoring a stop sign, and plowed into Bob's side of the car. The world spun, there was wrenching pain in my back, and Bob was lying on top of me.

I must have passed out for a moment because the next thing I remember I was standing in the street. Bob was sitting on the curbside, stunned but miraculously unhurt. The Chevrolet was lying on its side, the mangled passenger door facing the sky. Passersby had hauled us both out the shattered passenger window. The two men who had pulled me from the car tried to ease me down to the curb beside Bob, but the pain in my back made me yelp. A siren wailed, coming closer.

Another cluster of people was grouped around the driver of the other car. He too was on his feet, his car apparently undamaged. As the fog cleared from my head I saw that he was an elderly man and that the sobbing I heard was coming from him.

I tried to walk over to him to assure him that Bob and I were all right, but my rescuers held onto me. "Don't move! The ambulance is on the way!"

In addition to broken glass from my car windows, the street was littered with shards of pottery. It took me a minute to recognize the fragments of our wedding gifts.

Our wedding! I was on my way to be married and the rehearsal was this afternoon! I couldn't stand around like this. I tugged free from the men holding me and took a few faltering steps. My back felt like knives were turning in it but there didn't seem to be anything broken.

An ambulance screeched to the curb, roof light flashing,

and two white-jacketed men sprang out.

"I'm okay!" I protested, backing away. "You better take a look at the old fellow there."

But the other driver also refused to enter the ambulance, though tears were rolling down his face. I hobbled over to him.

"Don't feel bad, brother," I said. "God must have been looking out for all of us."

Then I looked closer. The old man's eyes were swollen, as though he'd been crying for hours. Two police cars were on the scene by now and the police started taking statements. The other driver had been returning from his wife's funeral. "Wouldn't go to the graveyard," he kept saying. "Couldn't watch them put her in the ground."

My heart went out to him, lonely, confused and heartbroken, and when the police wanted Bob and me to come down to the station and swear out charges against him, we declined. I carried insurance on the car, and though my back was plenty painful I was already walking better and Bob was not even scratched.

My only concern was somehow, someway, to get to McCook that afternoon. But one delay followed another until it was clear we would not get out of Lincoln that day. The police drove the old man home in his own car, but a tow truck had to be called to right the Chevrolet and haul it to a garage. Bob stayed to salvage any unbroken wedding gifts from the litter in the street, while I rode with the tow operator. It was a pain as acute as the one in my back to see my sleek red fastback dragged ignominiously by her rear axle, her side caved in, her windows shattered.

At the garage the grizzled mechanic took forever making an inventory of the damage. "Son," he said at last, "it'd take me a week to get this car on the road. If I had the parts. Which I don't. And the time, which I don't either."

I wrung from him a promise to get started as fast as he could on it, then began phoning everyone I knew who might let me borrow an automobile for the next two days. At last I reached my friend Walter Burns who agreed to let me take his 1937 Buick coupe as soon as his factory shift let out.

The last of a series of frantic calls to Betty: not to frighten her I'd said only that we were having car trouble. "We'll be on the road at daybreak," I promised. Then gratefully I put my back to bed.

I had hoped that a night's sleep would mend the damage, but next morning my spine was so stiff I had to roll from the bed to the floor. I limped down the front steps to where Walter was waiting with the car, while he and Bob speculated with what I thought was unnecessary hilarity on my upcoming wedding night.

When Bob and I reached the red brick church in McCook, Pastor Smitley and Reverend Alber were already waiting in the little room at the rear. While Bob and I changed into our suits they talked us hastily through the ceremony—where to stand, when to step forward, what to say.

The pianist began the wedding march and I hobbled painfully after the others into the church. On the platform an archway of white wrought iron had been erected and covered with ferns; wicker baskets on either side held white gladiolas. The sanctuary seated 350 and it was full.

Then Betty appeared in the doorway and I forgot my back, forgot that we had no car for our honeymoon trip, forgot everything but that God was giving me the girl who had stepped into the moonlight on an August night.

Patty preceded her down the aisle, wearing a long dress the color of lilacs. A few steps behind came Betty, walking alone. Lace covered her arms and her straight slender shoulders. A white veil hid her face and the train of her skirt shimmered as she walked. It was well I was moving stiffly or I might have forgotten Pastor Smitley's instructions and rushed up the aisle to meet her.

After the ceremony, there was a long, long reception. There were flowers and food and music and everyone but the groom seemed to have a marvelous time. It was evening when we climbed at last into the borrowed Buick, Betty and I . . . and

Bob Teague. I had cancelled the surprise reservation at the Brown Palace: without our car there was no way to get to Denver. All we could do was go back to Lincoln to wait for our car to be ready, and since Bob was going to Lincoln too, it seemed sensible to take him along.

The hours of standing had taken their toll on my back; after driving a short way I knew I would not make it to Lincoln that night. We stopped in the little town of Holdrege, Nebraska and carried our bags upstairs to a small hotel over a drugstore.

"Don't unpack your pretty things," I begged Betty. She and her mother had been sewing her trousseau for months. I hated the idea of inaugurating married life in this bare little room with Bob Teague on the other side of the paper-thin wall. "In just a few days," I promised, "we'll pick up our car and head for the mountains."

But a few days passed, then a week, then two weeks, and we were still in Lincoln. My back slowly recovered, but the car was another story. Instead of having my honeymoon with Betty, I seemed to be spending it in the garage. I pried names of suppliers from the uncommunicative old mechanic and spent hours on the phone trying to track down a door panel, a front fender, a radiator casing.

"Not going to do a particle of good," he predicted gloomily. "Factories just aren't turning out parts for private cars."

Not having the Chevrolet also meant we could not keep those speaking dates in the Colorado mountains. Camp meeting season had begun. While waiting for the car why not accept a few nearby engagements? I started phoning churches in the area. But summer programs had long since been finalized, speakers announced, schedules printed.

After a week of applying I located a meeting in Wichita Falls, Texas, where they needed a youth speaker and believed, through a member who worked for Greyhound, that they could get us aboard a bus. They did, as standees. All night and all the next day we clung to our hand-straps as the bus swayed south.

Texas in early June was the hottest place I'd ever been. Until we got to our next engagement: Lawrence, Kansas. Standards of dress for women, and especially wives of clergymen, were more conservative here than in Nebraska. Long sleeves and high necklines were expected, no matter how blistering the temperature. Betty accepted the adjustment as she had accepted the banishment of her make-up kit to the bottom of the suitcase. "After all, Charles, if a sleeveless dress and lipstick mean people can't hear the words I'm singing, what's the use in coming at all?"

In Dallas I was able to introduce her at last to my friend Gene Martin. Gene too was recently married, traveling with his wife, Ruth, as Betty and I were doing. While Gene and I spoke at churches in the area, Betty and Ruth enrolled in the Stamps-Baxter Music School for a two-week crash course in the accordion and the syncopated Southern style of gospel singing.

It was a wonderful summer after all, and by the end of it we had a full winter's worth of invitations to churches in 15 states, and every week of the following summer scheduled too. We were still traveling by bus and train, when we could get aboard, standing as often as we sat.

By September, when our car was still not repaired, we decided to sell it, though in its present condition it would not bring much. Since there were still no secondhand cars to be had, this meant getting on a long waiting list for a new one. We were ministering in a church in Salem, New Jersey, in February when word came that we could pick up our car in Lincoln. It was another Chevrolet, this time a sober green. "A really attractive shade," Betty said consolingly, knowing how much I had loved the red one.

We crisscrossed the country that spring and summer of 1944, from Wyoming to Florida, from California to Massachusetts, ministering at revivals, camp meetings, army bases, and by fall again had a full winter schedule of church dates. I was still reading a book a week as Reverend Alber had started me doing; a box in the back seat contained my slowly growing "library." There seemed no reason why Betty and I should not continue to travel and evangelize just as we were doing now for years to come.

And yet . . . especially when the drive had been a long one with two flat tires by night fall, we would talk about settling down. In May we had our second anniversary and started our third summer of journeying from one campground to another. The dishes and bedding which had survived the car crash were still in their boxes in a corner of the Rupperts' attic in McCook.

There were other things that were hard about evangelism, and the hardest was leaving people we had come to love. We would conduct meetings, see people come forward to have their lives changed, as I had come forward that night in Enid seven years ago, and then drive away.

"Wouldn't it be wonderful," Betty or I would say dreamily, "to be able to follow up with people! To see friends when we looked out at a congregation, instead of strangers. . . ." And then I'd be off, expounding my favorite theories on how to build a church. "We could do it anywhere," I'd say confidently.

But that was just the question. Of all the places we had worked, which one should we settle down in? We were in Spokane, Washington, when the news came that an atom bomb had been dropped on a place called Hiroshima. About that time we reached a decision. We'd been sending part of our offering money, of course, to Mrs. Ruppert, but in that closeknit threesome they needed one another's presence as well as each other's support.

"You know," Betty had cautioned me during our engagement, "when you get me, you're getting all three of us."

I did know, and I rejoiced. But getting to south central Nebraska from various parts of the country was something else.

"We'll live anywhere that fits your plans," Mrs. Ruppert told us. At the time we were married, however, Patty still had two years of high school to finish. In June she had graduated and now she was the most excited of any of us about moving. "Oh Charles, a real city, please! The bigger the better!"

"Somewhere where the dust doesn't blow so in the summer," Mother Ruppert suggested wistfully.

And: "Denver!" we all four said together. New, growing, centrally located between east and west, north and south—someday it would be an ideal place to settle. "Why," I said, "I bet I could build a church in Denver just like that!" And I snapped my fingers—which is a thing I have since learned never, never to do.

Meanwhile the city could be our headquarters, the stopover place between trips. And so in the fall of 1945 we bought a tiny white frame cottage for $3,800 in the suburb of Englewood and moved Mother and Patty there. It needed all kinds of things done to it, but the down payment was only $700 and most of the work we could do ourselves. All of us were so thrilled at having a place of our own after a lifetime of renting that it scarcely seemed like work. Every day Betty and I were home we were painting, papering, tearing out partitions, putting up shelves.

These moments were few and far between, though, as invitations to minister continued to come from all over the country. We were driving together through the South that November, on our way from a revival week in Atlanta to an air base near Mobile, when Betty turned in the front seat to face me.

"Charles, you remember that I wasn't sure? Well, now I am."

"You mean . . . you're . . . we're. . . ."

She nodded. I slammed on the brake and there in a pine woods we whooped and hugged each other and praised God.

The baby was due in June; in May we returned to Colorado to wait for the birth. There was a returning-servicemen's center in Colorado Springs, 65 miles south of Denver, where we volunteered our services, sleeping on cots in a back office. We were too far from Denver to leave the moment of birth to nature, so Betty chose the date for the induced labor: "If I go in after the Wednesday night service, I can be back to play the piano Sunday morning."

But childbirth, we were to discover, cannot be scheduled like a meeting. Wednesday night Betty's doctor started the injections, but this baby would not be hurried. When labor began at last it was a long and difficult one. All one day, all that night and all the following day Betty tossed on that hospital bed while I drove back and forth between Denver and Colorado Springs.

I was speaking to an overflow room of servicemen Sunday night, when word was whispered to me that our daughter Vicki had come. I don't believe the wheels of the Chevrolet touched the ground all the way to Denver.

Betty had planned to spend a few weeks in Englewood with her mother and Patty, but by the end of the week she and Vicki had joined me in Colorado Springs. "It just doesn't feel normal, putting my clothes in a drawer instead of a suitcase."

When the service center closed down in August with the mustering out of the men, we resumed our itinerant ministry, crossing and recrossing the country, but now with a baby in tow. Diapers, bottles, travel bed, the smallest member of the family seemed to have most of the luggage.

Now we prayed harder than ever to know God's direction for our lives. Invitations to pastor churches came from several parts of the country, and we felt drawn to them all. And yet, our traveling ministry had never been so active: many people assuring us we were anointed of God to be evangelists and not to pastor one church in one location.

In March, 1947, we stopped in Denver to pick up mail, praying as always over each letter we opened. The first was from a church in Cheyenne, Wyoming. They had been in prayer, the letter began, and had heard from God that we were to come to be their pastors. We were overwhelmed by their conviction.

But the next letter, from Mobile, Alabama, also reported that God had "told" them Betty and I were to pastor there. When the third proved to be from a congregation in Salem, New Jersey, who had unanimously received the word that we were to pastor *there,* both of us started to laugh. Obviously all these people were sincere, all had sought God's will, all believed they had found it. Equally obviously, they could not all be right—and neither, apparently, could we depend on other people's hearing God for us.

"Here's another that came just this morning." Mother Ruppert dropped an envelope on the kitchen table as she lifted Vicki out of her high chair. "I haven't rocked my granddaughter in weeks."

The postmark read "Edinburgh, Scotland." It was from a Reverend Robert Barrie; he was writing to invite us to lead a series of meetings at his church in June. "Why not come over in time for the international congress in Zurich in April?" He could set up speaking dates for me in England and France, which would help pay expenses.

The letter went on for three more pages but in my mind I had already left the little kitchen in Denver and was walking up the gangplank to the ship. "They want us! Over there. They've asked us to come!" I babbled to Betty.

Making no sense out of me, she took the letter and read it through. "Honey, why don't you go! You're obviously dying to!"

"Alone you mean? Without you? Never! It's both of us they want."

"But how could I possibly go? What about Vicki?"

"We'll take her with us!"

But this, when I simmered down enough to look at the facts, was not so simple. Postwar Europe with its shortages and uncertain travel was not the best place for a nine-month-old baby.

"You go," Betty repeated. "It'll only be a few months and Vicki and I'll have Mother and Patty and Don to keep us company." In August Patty had married a young Denver man just out of the Merchant Marines, Don Cooper.

"And who will I have to keep *me* company?"

So the conversation ranged: from neither of us going, to me going alone, to both of us going and leaving Vicki with Mother Ruppert who had overheard and joined us in the kitchen. "Of course you must go with him, Betty! I'll love having Vicki to myself—this house has been too lonesome since Patty moved out. Why it will be the honeymoon you never had!"

And if a honeymoon is the prelude to a different kind of life . . . honeymoon it surely was.

10

The next few days were a blurr of excitement—cancelling speaking dates around the country, selling the green Chevrolet to buy the boat tickets, corresponding with congregations in Europe whose names Pastor Barrie supplied. At the Cunard office in Denver I picked up a booklet titled *Tips for Travelers,* which I had all but memorized by the time we boarded the train at the end of the month.

Leaving Vicki was terrible; the train was out of Colorado before either of us could trust our voices to speak. Then gradually the excitement of our great adventure caught us up. When we walked across the gangplank with its red and white striped bunting onto the *Queen Elizabeth,* I wouldn't have traded places with anybody on earth.

We gawked at the huge tourist-class dining room like the greenhorns we were. Most of the tables seated eight or ten but beneath a porthole I spotted a small one for two. In Denver I had purchased some English money (*Tips for Travelers,* page 3) and now I drew a pound note from my pocket. "Could you put my wife and me at the table there?" I asked the tuxedoed head waiter.

"Certainly, sir. And I hope you enjoy your voyage with us."

As I watched him place a "Reserved" card on the table for two, I saw a newsboy venturing into the unimaginable splendor of the Youngblood Hotel coffee shop, gaping as Mr. Hawthorne left a tip on the counter. And now, I congratulated myself, I've tipped a British headwaiter and been "sirred" in response.

Alas for self-satisfaction: the ship was not even out of New York harbor before the first spasm of seasickness gripped me. By supper time I was flat on my bunk, wondering what had ever possessed me to venture away from solid land. Our cabin was in the bow of the ship, the cheapest location on board and the worst for motion sickness. I never once sat at the table for two by the porthole. By the second evening a sympathetic group at a nearby table, seeing her alone, had asked Betty to join them.

Europe, though, was everything we had dreamed. By the end of the first week our necks literally hurt from craning to see everything at once. *Tips for Travelers* led us to a hotel in Paris within our budget. The elevator was a tiny wire cage in an open well: Betty gave the thing one look and climbed the five flights to our room.

It was the only time we stayed in a hotel. Our first preaching date was in a small church just outside the city, where we stayed at the pastor's house, learning to communicate with gestures and smiles. Out of a scrawny chicken and a few potatoes the pastor's wife put on the table a delectable dinner. Everywhere we went in war-ravaged France the people turned shortages into an immense and gay-hearted creativity.

How my sermons came across through the mouths of various translators I could only guess, but they were received with touching eagerness, possibly because we came from the land that stood for hope and abundance. As for the rhythmic Southern style of gospel music which Betty had learned in Dallas, it created a sensation in postwar Europe. Word of our coming leapt from town to town and we held morning, noon and evening services until the last possible train to the Zurich convention.

And in Zurich we were given the vision which has never faded from that day to this. The vision of the Body of Christ. Here were brothers and sisters from every corner of the world—Africa, Asia, South America, as well as every part of Europe—all worshiping the same Lord who had found and saved us in Oklahoma and Nebraska, USA. At every meeting, at every meal, we met church leaders eager to bring their people "the American viewpoint."

"When you come to South Africa you must stay with us in Durban."

". . . speak to our people in Stockholm."

". . . meetings right across Australia."

". . . a six-week campaign in Berlin."

Dazed by the ministry I saw forming before my eyes, I said yes to them all. After the week with Pastor Barrie in Edinburgh in June, we'd continue on to Scandinavia and Germany. Then home to pick up Vicki. Shortages should be easier by the coming fall, everyone said; host churches would see to it that there was milk for her.

And then . . . the world before us! Five years? Ten years? Going where the Spirit led to hungry and receptive congregations everywhere. . . .

From Switzerland we traveled through Italy, then back across Europe. *Si, oui oui, ja,* we'd be back, very soon! Rome, Florence, Paris—how clear it was that God had called to these stimulating and important places.

Then England: London, Leeds, Birmingham, the Hippodrome in Manchester—we had to pinch ourselves to believe that Charles and Betty Blair from Nebraska were sitting on platforms with men like J. Nelson Parr and Donald Gee, men whose books had traveled in the back seat of the green Chevrolet.

At the train station in Edinburgh, a sandy-haired man in his 40s introduced himself as Robert Barrie. Edinburgh was even smokier than Minneapolis, but to Betty and me it was the essence of romance, with the great bulk of the castle dominating the city. The Barries put us in a room with a four-poster bed and an antarctic temperature. There was a coal-burning fireplace in one wall, but on account of the war no coal to put in it. They gave us an electric kettle and a teapot with a hand-knit woolen cozy and we drank hot tea until our teeth were stained brown.

The meetings at Pastor Barrie's church lasted for a week, the nightly services opening with glorious Scottish singing. Daytimes, Betty and I roamed the streets where so many heroes of the faith had walked—Knox, Calvin, our own Puritan fathers—and learned to eat fish and chips out of newspaper folded into cones.

Saturday morning we were brewing our third pot of tea when Dr. Barrie rapped on the door. "Cablegram for you—just come from the States."

Vicki went through both our minds as I tore it open. But after all it turned out to be only another invitation to pastor a Stateside church. "One more case," I said to Betty with a smile, "of people 'hearing' from God."

This time the church was in Denver, and of all the groups who "knew" that we were to come and be their pastors, it was by far the smallest. "Listen to this," I said to Betty. *"All 32 members voted you pastor effective immediately advise acceptance."*

Thirty-two members! In the boom atmosphere of postwar Europe Betty and I had stopped thinking in terms even of hundreds: attendance at most meetings was reckoned to the nearest thousand.

I glanced at the name on the cable. Central Assembly. Sure—I remembered them. Church had been designed as a movie theater. Well, it was nice of them to think of us, but with the whole world beckoning, pastoring a church back in our own home town had little appeal.

"If you need to send an answer," said Dr. Barrie, "I'm walking downtown later and can point out the wireless office."

So that afternoon I accompanied him down the beautiful

boulevard called Princes Street. The sidewalk was thronged with uniformed school children and nannies pushing red-cheeked babies in high-wheeled prams. Pigeons too: there must have been a thousand birds soaring and wheeling about us as I wrestled with the wording of the cable. Overseas messages were charged by the word; how could I be brief, yet courteous? At last I settled on: *Regret European commitments prevent accepting nomination.* Six words, plus the signature and the address: *Central Assembly, 4th and Grant, Denver, Colorado, USA.* Fourteen words in all.

"The cable office is in the next block," Dr. Barrie said. "Why, what's wrong, Charles?"

I had stopped dead still in the middle of the crowded sidewalk. Around us nothing had changed—hurrying people, wheeling birds. But inside, the world had done a flip-flop.

"Is anything wrong?" Dr. Barrie said again.

"No. That is—Dr. Barrie, I feel as though there was a brick wall right across this sidewalk."

A lady pushing twins in a wicker carriage said, "Beg pardon!" and we stepped hastily to one side.

"Have you ever felt—" I struggled to express the sensation I was having. "A kind of 'stop' signal inside? Almost like a warning. *Careful! You're about to make a mistake!*"

"Many times," the Scotsman said. "And when I do I've learned to listen to what the Holy Spirit may be trying to tell me.

"You know, Charles," he added, "I wasn't planning to say anything, as it's none of my business, but it did strike me as odd that you and Betty never prayed about that cablegram this morning."

Well, no, we hadn't. But . . . some things were obvious, weren't they? I mean, a struggling church in a Stateside city, when all the excitement today was overseas—what was there to pray about?

But the strange pressure in my spirit continued. Betty was as puzzled as I when I told her I had not sent the cable. "Charles, don't we owe them a reply, out of courtesy? Since you know you'll never take that job, is it fair to keep them waiting?"

Sunday afternoon was the final service in Pastor Barrie's church. The sanctuary was packed, the joy and power of the Spirit something you could almost touch. By the closing prayers, the mood of worship was too strong to stay in our seats. Without a word of suggestion, the entire congregation got on its knees, turning to face the pews, while those of us on the platform knelt facing our chairs.

Thus Betty, in the main body of the church, and I on the platform, had our backs to each other when a man near the rear of the sanctuary—I never saw who—spoke two sentences in a rolling Scots accent:

"I have set before you an open door which no man will be able to shut. If you will walk through it in obedience I will bless you in so much that men will be amazed and glorify God!"

As clearly as if my name had been spoken, I knew that those words in the mouth of a stranger were God's words to me—and that the door He had opened was at 4th Street and Grant in Denver, Colorado. Not Scandinavia or South Africa or Australia or any of the other doors I had been gleefully peering through, but this totally unasked-for, seemingly least promising one of all.

The experience was so strong, and so directly contrary to every idea and plan of my own, that I straightened and looked around. Dr. Barrie and the church elders continued to pray, faces buried in the red velvet of the chair seats. Still kneeling, I turned and looked out over the congregation.

And at that moment Betty too turned around. Our eyes met and, in that incredible instant, I knew that she had heard exactly what I had heard.

Monday morning we cabled our acceptance to Central Assembly, then spent the rest of the day writing letters: "God has called us to Denver and we must therefore regretfully cancel our visit to. . . ." "Betty and I looked forward so much to joining you in July but God has called us to Denver and. . . .

God has called us to Denver—though I wrote the words again and again they shocked me each time. We'd been so sure that He was calling us to the whole world!

But now that we had heard His voice, our role was not only to obey, but to obey at once. *Immediately* the cablegram said, but I sensed that there was more than human scheduling behind the urgency I felt to step through the door that God Himself had opened. The thought of fjords and midnight sun—all the excitement I'd felt about traveling later in the week to Scandinavia—had vanished like mist in the sun. The whole world seemed colorless except the spot where God's light was shining for us.

I knew our guidance had to be genuine when Betty agreed that we should try to get plane tickets. I'd made a couple of short flights in the States, but she had never flown and often declared she never would. And in any case we'd never get aboard. There were very few flights across the Atlantic in 1947 and those few, especially now in June, booked solid.

Nevertheless I went to a travel agency on Princes Street. There was a long wait in the usual orderly queue, but at last a clerk was free. "My wife and I would like to change two boat tickets to New York next month for plane tickets leaving right away."

The man shook his head decisively, "We can't get you on a plane until September."

The line behind me was growing; I should have left the counter. "No flights to New York at all?" I echoed stupidly.

The clerk in the next position turned to stare at me. "Did you say New York?" he asked. He indicated the couple standing in front of him. "These people are trying to sell two seats on the flight from Glasgow tomorrow night."

When Betty saw the plane tickets actually in my hand, the color drained from her face. To have her very first flight across an ocean. . . .

At midnight Tuesday we boarded the plane in Glasgow. As the propellers jerked into motion, I saw Betty's lips begin to move. I leaned closer. She was whispering the words of a hymn:

Fear thou not for I'll be with thee
I will still thy pilot be . . .

From New York Thursday morning we boarded a train for Denver. Our plan had been to fly the rest of the way, too, but after changing our pounds back into dollars we discovered we did not have enough for plane tickets. I could see Betty praising God for poverty clear across the country.

We'd figured our finances so close, in fact, that there was barely enough for meals en route. In Chicago there was a long wait between trains; we wandered hungrily along a street of restaurants reading the menus till we found one featuring a spaghetti plate.

It was a jolting plunge from abundance—packed meetings, generous collections and bargain prices for Americans carrying dollars—to the kind of scrimping I was all too familiar with. And there'll be a lot more of it, I reminded myself as the train wheels clacked beneath us, starting out with a small, struggling church.

For a fleeting moment I allowed myself to wish that we hadn't been quite as freehanded with the money that had flowed through our fingers in Europe. But that was a principle about money that I had learned in the first church I had ever entered. "God gives us money to use, not to keep," Lloyd Johnson would say. "He wants us to become channels of His supply. As long as our channels are open to others, there will always be enough. But the minute we try to seal them off, to accumulate the flow for ourselves, it will cease."

These months in Europe offerings had overflowed—and so had the need in those war-torn lands. With bed and meals provided wherever we went, it never occurred to us to hold back some of the offerings for ourselves.

I earnestly hoped I would have done the same had I known how soon we'd be going home; still it was an embarrassment, when we stepped off the train in Denver Friday morning, to reach in my pocket and discover I didn't even have taxi fare to

Englewood. There was no other way to get there with our luggage and so our homecoming began with me dashing into the house calling, "Mother Ruppert! Can I borrow some money?"

Betty scooped up our little girl while I dashed back to the waiting driver.

Only then did I let myself reach for my daughter. It was June 22, Vicki's first birthday. We were home. We were broke. We were on the threshold of a life so different, so difficult, that had I known what lay ahead I think I would have run after that taxi and begged our way back to Europe.

11

There was no hint of trouble to come that first Sunday morning. No longer owning a car, it was once more a taxi which let Betty, Mother Ruppert, Vicki and me off at 4th Street and Grant, five minutes from the state capitol. The stuccoed church was on the corner, a filling station next door. The elders of the little congregation were waiting on the steps to greet us and show us around. The fan-shaped sanctuary with its folding blond opera seats showed its origin as a movie house. "It seats four hundred," one of the men told us, obviously embarrassed at so large a plant for so small a congregation. "Room to grow, you see."

The theater lobby made a handsome entrance foyer and a small room off this, which had been the movie manager's office, was now the "pastor's study." At the rear of the sanctuary a door led onto a stairway. Up four steps was a second door, which an elder threw open. "Your kitchen!" he announced.

I saw Betty look dubiously at the tiny cubicle: a stove, sink and refrigerator filled it. An L-shaped living-dining room, two small bedrooms and a bathroom completed the apartment. The bedroom windows faced the white stucco wall of a garage belonging to an apartment house next door and I knew Betty was thinking of the yard outside our house in Englewood.

Down in the sanctuary the congregation was assembling. Counting everybody, members, teenagers, children, friends of members, casual visitors and babies Vicki's age, there were perhaps 100 people present that first Sunday. It was the spirit not the number which excited us, a sense of expectancy that reached out to embrace us and sweep away any lingering doubts about our call. From the pulpit I described that service in Edinburgh when Betty and I had known for sure.

"God was there in Edinburgh," I concluded triumphantly, "and He's here in Denver this morning."

A few days later we moved out of the little house in Englewood; Betty and I had never spent a full week in our first home. An immediate benefit of the sale was that we were able once again to buy a car.

A harder job was fitting the four of us into the apartment at church. Vicki was a light sleeper. In a room by herself she was fine, but let someone tiptoe in—or even touch the doorknob to her room—and she would wake and cry.

I came upstairs at lunch time one day, after a morning in my small office off the lobby, to find Betty putting Vicki down for her nap in a strangely altered bedroom.

"Where's Mother Ruppert's bed?" I asked.

"In the basement," Betty said helplessly. "You talk to her, Charles! I've said everything I know how to."

I raced back through the kitchen and down the stairs, past the door to the sanctuary and on down the backless wooden steps to the cellar. There next to the furnace which heated the church, and the big zinc washtub where Betty did the laundry, Mother was arranging her clothes in a chest-of-drawers. She'd gotten the young people's group to carry it and her bed down the basement stairs.

"Mother! You can't live down here!"

"And why not, Charles Blair?"

"Well, it's underground for one thing." There was only one

tiny window high in the wall. "There's no light!"

"I won't hear another word, Charles. There's running water and privacy, and I won't be down here except at night."

Nothing any of us said was able to budge her from her decision. And in fact she spent little time there. She was needed not only to care for Vicki while Betty played for the various services, but around the building which I, in my preoccupation with sermons and pew counts, scarcely noticed. I took it for granted that the carpeting in the aisle would be vacuumed, the chair backs dusted. It was weeks before it penetrated my skull that my petite and ladylike mother-in-law had appointed herself unofficial—and certainly unpaid—church janitor.

Betty too was occupied from morning till night: washing, ironing, cooking, caring for the apartment and Vicki, helping with the choir, teaching Sunday school, leading Bible studies.

Only one member of the family seemed to find time heavy on his hands. . . . Every statistic I could get hold of indicated that Denver was the ideal field for the kind of mass evangelistic outreach I had in mind. Unlike "Bible belt" towns, most families in this fast-growing city were unchurched. Nor did there seem to be any vigorous effort to reach them. On paper anyhow it looked as though Denver was right for the kind of witness Betty and I could offer. But calculations on paper did not equal faces in the pews. Sunday after Sunday I preached the most soul-winning sermons I knew how—to the sound of the traffic on Grant Street whizzing past.

One Monday evening in June, 1948, 12 months after we'd cancelled our travel plans and rushed here from Scotland, I sat in my cubbyhole of a study and took stock. Had Betty and I heard God in Edinburgh? I was convinced that we had. Had we done our very best for a year now? Yes, again. Why, then, were people not flocking to Central Assembly? I continued to be invited to speak in other parts of the country and everywhere else my message was received with excitement. Crowds turned out, hundreds made decision for Christ.

The problem, obviously, was Denver. And a full year of

trying was enough. I took a piece of stationery from the desk drawer and began to work on my letter of resignation. It took several drafts until I was satisfied. Along with my reasons for resigning I wanted to express my gratitude to the faithful few who had given us such love and support. At last I carried the letter across the sanctuary, smelling of the polish Mother Ruppert used weekly on the pulpit, through the door at the rear of the platform and up the stairs. Betty was doing the dishes.

"I want to read something to you," I said, standing in the doorway because there wasn't room for both of us at the sink.

For a while after I finished there was only the sound of swishing in the dishpan. One by one Betty set the dishes on the drainboard. Then she wiped her hands and turned to face me. The curve beneath her apron reminded me that our second child was due in three months. She was so beautiful at that moment that I longed to forget about church growth and membership drives and take her in my arms.

"Charles," she said, "I'm disappointed in you. I don't believe people in Denver are one bit different from people anywhere. If you can't build a church here, you can't do it anywhere!"

That was more or less what she said. The only words I really heard were those first ones. *I'm disappointed in you.* All my childhood sense of inferiority, my fear of being looked down upon, came rushing to the surface with those words. For years I'd kept them down with the right clothes, the right car, the right words. And now I had failed. Worse, I had been seen to fail by the person whose good opinion I most longed for. Betty now saw me as I secretly feared myself to be. A loser. A laughingstock. The boy with the milk pail.

I plunged back down the stairway. Four steps down—don't think about the fact that you haven't been able to provide her mother with anything but a basement hole to live in. Into the sanctuary—don't see most of these seats empty Sunday after Sunday. Through the lobby and into my office.

And there in that room I got down on my knees and asked

God to show me how to build a church. His glory and my glory, Betty's opinion of me and Claudia Williams' opinion, were all jumbled together in that prayer. But when I got to my feet, hours later, it was with the certainty that He had heard me, mixed motives and all. And that, though my reasons for sticking with this little church on the corner of 4th Street and Grant were still all wrapped up with self, His reasons for putting me here were as sovereign—and as mysterious—as ever.

It was the following week that a strange idea popped into my mind. I was reading a collection of sermons by the renowned Tennessee preacher Dr. Robert G. Lee. On the dust jacket was a photograph of a tall distinguished-looking man in his mid-fifties standing in front of a stately white-columned building which the caption identified as "the 5,000-member Bellevue Baptist Church of Memphis." Five thousand members!

What, I thought suddenly, if I were to write Dr. Lee and ask him how he had achieved this incredible figure?

And so, feeling presumptuous and excited both at once, I wrote a long letter telling him that I was a 27-year-old minister with a small congregation, and asking if I might come to visit him. I didn't really expect an answer, but to my surprise one arrived: by all means I must come to Memphis.

And so on a Sunday night in July, after the evening service at Central Assembly, I boarded a train for Tennessee. The following afternoon, hot and rumpled from the long sit-up journey, I climbed down the steps at the Memphis station to see on the platform the very man whose picture was on the book. There must have been a large staff at Bellevue Baptist, but Dr. Lee himself had come to the station to meet a total stranger.

He had a couple of stops to make, he apologized, as we climbed into his car. The "couple of stops" turned out to be six leisurely visits with parishioners and nonparishioners alike. He seemed infinitely involved with each of them, asking by name about children, a recent vacation, "how's that sore shoulder?"

Dr. Lee's home, when we reached it at last, was everything

I had imagined a Southern mansion to be. There was little time to enjoy the surroundings, however. After supper Dr. Lee got out his car again. Tonight the calls were in the suburbs: a family of nine, and an old man living alone; a country estate where a butler opened the door, and a rundown farm with a well and pump in the yard.

I stayed with the Lees five days and saw their gracious porticoed home only at bedtime. In between we called on the sick, the elderly, the newcomer, the housebound young mother. Driving from one appointment to the next I would tell him about my problems trying to reach Denver for the Lord. "I think out West people are more material-minded, Dr. Lee. They're always in a hurry."

He bore with me for several days. Then one afternoon returning from a visit south of town he turned his car into a pullout overlooking the wide brown Mississippi.

"You keep talking about reaching Denver," he began. "Son, God doesn't know anything about reaching cities. When He was on earth He reached individuals. And that's how He seeks and finds us today."

He waved a hand toward the Memphis skyline. "He didn't install Himself in a synagogue in some Judean city and wait for people to come and hear the truth. He went where the people were, into their homes and streets and places of business. He found them where they were hurting, and He began with that."

He *went*. . . . As though a spotlight had been turned on, I saw myself hanging out my shingle at the corner of 4th and Grant: Charles Blair is here! And then sitting back to wait for an eager world to find its way to me. If people had turned out to hear me during my years as a traveling evangelist I saw, in that light's unflattering glare, it was because other men—the true pastors—had sought and found them already, one by one as I had watched Dr. Lee do this past week, and brought each to the place where he was interested in what a passing evangelist might have to say.

It was not until I was riding home on the train that I realized that I had not once talked with Dr. Lee about how to write a sermon. That was what I had supposed his great secret to be. And yet this brilliant preacher whose sermons were studied in seminaries all over the country, had put no emphasis at all on the pulpit. *Get out where the people are,* was his message. *Visit the sick, the friendless, the lonely. . . .*

The very next week Betty and I began putting his advice into practice. One day she would take the car while I made calls along the bus and streetcar routes; next day we'd reverse it. We called on everyone who'd ever signed a visitor's card. We called on their friends and the friends of their friends.

The response astonished us. We recruited others in our small corps of church members to go with us, a man with me, a lady with Betty. Soon there were half-a-dozen such teams fanning out across the city, discovering as we went the enormity of the problems people were carrying silently and alone.

Looking back, years later, during the crisis, I wondered how such a program could have gone wrong. I'd go to directors of hospitals around the city, offering my services to any patient who did not have a clergyman of his own. In 1948 few hospitals had full-time chaplains and my offer was met with almost pathetic eagerness. It was the old people I loved visiting most. So often I was the only caller from one week to the next. When they were discharged I started going to the various nursing homes they were transferred to. How cheerless most of these places were!

Along with the face-to-face visiting, Betty and I started a daily radio outreach, which proved the most effective "going where the people are" of all. One noon a young Mexican American rapped on our kitchen door. His grandmother was dying, he told us in labored English.

In my car he directed me to an unheated shack. On a tattered mattress on the floor lay an old lady, a younger woman cradling her head.

"She's afraid to die," the younger one explained to me. "She heard you pray on the radio and she wants you to say a prayer for her."

I knelt on the rugless floor and took the large-knuckled hands in my own. Then with the daughter translating, I told a 92-year-old lady about the love of Jesus which had cancelled out the things in her life that made her afraid to die. The look on that dignified and wrinkled face when she accepted Him as her Savior, the utter peace in her half-blind eyes, gave me as much joy as any sermon I'd ever preached.

There were so many such episodes that Betty and I knew we must never again be without a radio outreach. So important did that daily program seem to us that Betty—ever disciplined—arranged once more to have an induced labor. "If I have the baby Thursday I'll only have to miss two broadcasts."

And this time all went according to plan: at nine o'clock Monday morning, September 28, Betty was seated again at the organ, playing the opening hymn of the broadcast, while upstairs Mother Ruppert and Vicki watched over four-day-old Judy.

Judy had the same golden hair, the same wide-set blue eyes as her big sister. Vicki adored her. On her third birthday, when Judy was nine months old, the only guest Vicki would have at her party was "my own sister."

Meanwhile I had made the second of the two trips which were to set the course of my ministry. Emboldened by Dr. Lee's kindness to me, I had written to another man whose career embodied everything I admired. This was Dr. Louis Evans, pastor of the famous Hollywood Presbyterian Church in Los Angeles. Dr. Evans too agreed to see me.

"You say you want to know how we manage to attract such a large congregation here at Hollywood Presbyterian," he repeated when I had sat down across from his great mahogany desk. "Young man, attracting is the easy part. There are all kinds of ways to do it. Newspaper ads, posters—your radio show's as good a method as any. But, Charles, all the ballyhoo in the world doesn't solve the real problem. How do you keep people coming back, after that first time?"

He got up and walked to the window overlooking a stone courtyard. "Some ministers," he said, "spend all their time telling people that they need a Savior."

I thought of the soul-winning sermons into which I poured myself week after week.

"But after his hearers have taken that step," Dr. Evans went on, "if he then doesn't give their newborn souls what they need to grow on, those people are going to keep moving. They've got to have nourishment and they'll keep looking until they find it."

It was another of those moments when a spotlight goes on. It shone on me mounting the platform Sunday after Sunday to preach salvation to people who were already saved. I was still an evangelist; I had not yet become a nurturer. I'd been standing at the door of the sheepfold calling out, *In here is life, joy, health!* But then when people came in, I failed to show them that life.

"How do you do it?" I asked Dr. Evans. "How do you get the food yourself to keep on feeding people?"

By living, he answered in essence. By sharing your life with others and learning from them. "And, of course, by reading." He waved an arm at his floor-to-ceiling shelves. "I would estimate," he said—and then he made the remark that has governed my daily schedule ever since—"I would estimate that for every minute I spend in the pulpit I spend an hour studying."

An hour of reading for every minute of preaching. A ratio of sixty to one. And I had thought because I read a book a week I had done my homework.

Over the next few months my sermons changed. I knew they were different by the different reactions at the door. Not the "Wow! That was powerful!" that the evangelist loves to hear, but "You've given me a lot to think about," or "That touched on the very thing that's been troubling me."

Over the months, too, the difference began to be reflected in attendance. There was never a spectacular increase in any one month or year, just a steady dependable growth, year in, year out. Growth in numbers soon ceased to be the goal either of the preaching or the visiting. I used, in fact, to request the names of the very elderly or very handicapped—people who couldn't possibly come to church—for my own calling. I didn't understand it. I only knew that to step into the room where a very old man or woman sat—sometimes sightless, sometimes witless, often in the drabbest, most pitiful surroundings—filled me with indescribable love that had to be God's own.

Following my visits with Dr. Lee and Dr. Evans, however, the church did begin to grow. By 1949 the 400-seat sanctuary was filled each Sunday and we started holding a second service, then a third. By 1950 we were borrowing rooms for Sunday school classes all over the neighborhood.

And it was also in 1950 that I learned a lesson which—had I but paid attention—could have kept us from the disaster ahead.

In 1950 the full picture of postwar need in the Far East was beginning to reach Western countries. And so Central Assembly sent me to the Orient to see what part we could play in the answer. I traveled with two other ministers, Lester Sumrall from South Bend, Indiana, and Ernie Reb from Tulsa, Oklahoma. What we discovered was suffering of a kind we'd never dreamed of. Starvation, disease, misery on a scale that demanded not only our money but our lives. After long nights of prayer we asked God to guide us to the cities where He wanted each to go. Lester was given a concern for Hong Kong, Ernie for Calcutta, I for Manila; we went home to resign our churches and offer ourselves to our respective mission boards.

When I told Betty of the certainty I felt, she was silent for a while. I followed her eyes from two-year-old Judy to four-year-old Vicki, in identical white organdy pinafores. I knew she was wondering what kind of life our little girls would have in Manila. Then there was the house started in my absence! The church had long since run out of classroom space, and one logical place to expand was into our apartment. But this meant finding somewhere for us to live. A carpenter who was a member of the church volunteered to build a house for us, if we would supply plans. We couldn't afford to hire them done, so Betty became both architect and contractor. When I left for the Pacific she was bent over plumbers' catalogs and electricians' diagrams.

Now, just as the mason was scheduled to pour the foundation on our small lot at 3rd and Vine, I arrived back with the news that we were called to the Philippines. "But if that's what God wants," Betty said at last, as I had known she would, "then I want it too."

The church also agreed that we must follow God's leading. We heard that Lester and Ernie had both been accepted by their mission boards. Ours was the slowest to respond but at last their approval came too. We were excited when we learned that the head of the Foreign Mission Department, Noel Perkin himself, was coming to sign us up.

"Choose a nice restaurant for our meeting," he instructed. "You won't have many luxuries once you get to the Philippines."

We selected the Tiffin in its romantic old house at 16th and Ogden, a table for three in the corner where Betty and I could listen to our new director's instructions. But over the soup Mr. Perkin was silent.

"I had the strangest experience coming here on the plane," he said at last in a mystified voice. "As I wrote you, we were delighted to receive an application from a young family with experience in a pastorate. You seemed tailor-made for Manila.

"But on the plane God began speaking to me. He said, 'I have put the Blairs in Denver and that is where I want them. They are not to leave.' "

He laid down his fork and looked from one of us to the other. "He seemed to be saying, Betty, Charles: 'I care for My children in Manila and I have made provision for them. To the Blairs I have given another job.'

"I don't understand it," Mr. Perkin confessed. "I only know that it isn't the need we see around us that should dictate our actions, it's finding God's will in each instance."

"If it were only the need," he went on, "every Christian should go at once to Manila, and that obviously couldn't work. Who knows, Charles and Betty, maybe you'll do more for the Philippines by staying here and building a church that can support half a dozen missionaries. . . ."

We put Mr. Perkin on his return flight with a mixture of emotions. Shock, puzzlement, a sense of deflation. "You mustn't rely on my guidance alone," Mr. Perkin had cautioned; indeed if there was one thing we had learned when seeking a church to pastor, it was that you couldn't depend on hearing from God through other people. So we set about again to pray, to read Scripture, to listen. Our whole congregation prayed with us. Over the weeks the word Mr. Perkin had heard on the plane was confirmed. And over the years it has been reconfirmed. The call to Asia was for Ernie Reb and Lester Sumrall; I had mistaken their guidance for mine. Both of these men were to spend 20 years of superlative ministry in the Orient; I was one of those called to stay at home. In Scotland I had heard God's voice say *Go!* In Denver I was learning to hear when He said *Stay.*

I was to stay in part so that I could form a support team behind missionary heroes on the front. Foreign missions became the great, overriding concern of our church. By the end of the decade we were supporting not the half-dozen missionaries Mr. Perkin foresaw, but five times that number, in Africa and South America and the Near East as well as in Asia. We were helping to build churches and hospitals, schools and radio stations over all the world and seeing young people from our own congregation stand up to volunteer for the field.

It isn't the need we see that tells us what to do; it's finding God's will for our particular lives.

I was seeing this principle at work so clearly. How was it possible that I would so soon forget it?

12

I should have known that the principle of laying aside our own programs was fundamental to the Christian walk. The house at 3rd and Vine, for example. Betty had truly, with her whole heart, given it up to obey that call to the Philippines. When God kept us instead in Denver, our new house was given back to us and became our joyful home for many years. My only disappointment was that Dad and Mother had never seen it. My brother Bob had a church of his own now, down in Tucson, Arizona; our families would visit back and forth. Bertha Mae was married to a pastor in Ogden, Utah; frequently she and her husband would stop to see us. But by 1955 we'd been in Denver eight years and Mother and Dad had never once come to visit. When we wanted to see them Betty and the girls and I would make the drive to Oklahoma. We would find Mother and Dad in some sun-parched bungalow, their rust-eaten automobile parked in the yard.

"They're happy as prairie larks," Betty would reproach me when I fretted over the way they lived. "They're serving God, they love each other. Why can't you enjoy them the way they are?"

Because—I suppose—I wanted them to enjoy *my* way of life

too. I wanted them to be proud of me.

I was especially sorry when in 1955 they once more declined to come for a visit. Because this year we had not only our home on Vine Street to show them, but another answer to prayer so overwhelming, so glorious that every time I drove past it I wanted to shout for joy.

Four years earlier, back in 1951, we had faced the fact that the church building at 4th and Grant was simply not adequate for the ministry we were being given. At each of the three services the 400-seat auditorium overflowed, with so many people sitting in the aisles that the fire department sent a warning. Parking was a nightmare, finding room for 40 Sunday school classes harder still.

At first we thought of tearing down the church and putting up a larger building right where we were. But the incredible picture that kept coming to us as we prayed was a sanctuary to seat one thousand! There would never be room on the present lot, and so we had divided a map of the city into quarters and assigned a committee to explore each one for building sites. Several were available but the price was always out of the question. We were still not a large congregation and certainly not a wealthy one. Store clerks, typists, laborers, a few doctors and teachers—most of us were people on modest salaries, excited but frightened, too, at the size of the vision God had given us.

At last we found a block of rundown small homes built on land that bordered the former city dump. The empty or neglected houses could all be bought, we believed, for not too much. Vicki was in the first grade at Bromwell School and when I picked her up the two of us would walk home that way. There were nine houses and one vacant lot making up a city block. Round and round it Vicki and I would march: "Lord, is this the land You are giving us?" It certainly seemed ideal: more centrally located than our present church, and on major bus routes. Best of all, across the street ground was being broken for a "shopping center"—at that time a revolutionary new idea.

Diffidently I approached the developer. Of course, he assured me, the church would be welcome to use their parking lot without charge on Sunday mornings. When the homes were torn down, we calculated, we'd own nearly three acres; with parking space already provided, that would be plenty of room for that still-unbelievable thousand-seat sanctuary and an educational wing alongside.

The more we prayed about it the more the entire congregation got the same answer—this is God's spot! So began the months-long process of buying the nine houses and the vacant lot. Supported in prayer, real estate people in the congregation reported their progress week after week. In June, 1952, the great day came when we announced to the newspapers that our little church would build a large new sanctuary at First Avenue and University. "Non-denominational." I stressed to the reporters; some while back we'd dropped our official ties with the Assemblies of God. The name we chose for the planned church building was Calvary Temple. "Calvary" to remind us that only His sacrifice made any achievement on our part possible. "Temple" because we wanted His praise to ascend without ceasing from the new building.

Papers carried the story on a Tuesday. Wednesday morning the phone rang in my little study off the vestibule at 4th and Grant. "The Reverend Charles E. Blair? One moment, please, I have a call from Chicago."

A pause, then a man's voice: "Blair? Is this the Blair who's bought up that block in Denver?" He was calling, he informed me, on behalf of Sears Roebuck and Company. It seemed that Sears was considering an enormous Denver store adjacent to the new shopping center. They were interested in the property we now owned. Couldn't they find us a similar piece of land elsewhere?

After all our searching, all our prayer? "I'm sorry, sir, we feel that this is the location God has given us."

The next day the Sears representative was on the phone again. They would not only locate a comparable piece of property for us, they would throw in $10,000 for any inconvenience caused. I felt duty bound to report the proposal to the congregation that Sunday, but no one felt right about it. We were through looking; an architect was already drawing up plans for the block on First and University.

It was a week or two later that the experience happened.

I was driving home along University Boulevard when my eyes were drawn to a large vacant meadow. I pulled the car to the curb and sat staring at it; ten acres at least of untouched and level land.

I got out of the car and tramped through the tall weeds in the fading light, my heart thumping strangely against my ribs. How was it possible that our committees could have passed this lovely field without seeing it? It was just two blocks south of our new site at First and University, and next door to one of the finest residential sections of the city. Clearly the reason none of us had ever noticed this property was that it was too big, too beautiful, too far above our highest sights. But the thought now hammering wildly against my chest was:

"Calvary Temple will stand here."

As darkness fell I got down on my knees in that tall grass: "Lord, if this is Your voice, let me not be afraid to listen."

The reaction of the site committees at church was as startled as my own: not one person had noticed this overgrown field. The Sears agent was unfamiliar with the property too. "But I can find out who owns it."

He called back the next day. The land was owned by the State of Colorado and it was not for sale. "It was one of the places they were considering for the Governor's Mansion."

"But they're not going to build there?"

"No, but they wouldn't even discuss selling. It's residential zoning anyway."

"Churches qualify as residential use," I reminded him.

There was a silence. "I'll get back to you," he said.

And back he called, day after day, week after week. He came up with one piece of property after another to swap for ours, and each time the cash they offered as an incentive was increased. It began to dawn on us that our block at First and University must be very central to their Denver plans.

"That property at University and Alameda," he said one day, "the one you're interested in? The state seems to believe we're only using your church as a way around the zoning. Would you testify that a church would actually be built on this site?"

And so I went to the capitol and described our great dream. And on a bright cold day in late fall the Sears purchasing agent, in exchange for our original block, presented our building committee with the deed to property three times as large and a check for $68,000.

We passed those bits of paper from hand to hand, stunned at what God had done. There was no way on earth our small congregation could have approached the State of Colorado about that property. Only a giant like Sears, with its legal knowhow and bluechip credit could even have asked the right questions.

God knew too what we did not know about the original block at First and University: that Denver's new one-way street system was shortly going to cut it exactly in half, leaving a small island of green in an intersection of busy thoroughfares. Sears, with its many adjacent blocks was able to utilize the remaining half-block, and also to take advantage of the improved traffic flow.

Nor had it even crossed our minds in the early 50s—though of course, again, God knew—that stores in Denver were going to start opening on Sundays. There would have been no parking available for the church at all. . . .

Looking back, we saw that God had guided us to that original block not because He wanted a church there, but as the only way to get around the smallness of our thinking. When we first decided to move from 4th and Grant a thousand-seat auditorium had seemed preposterously large. Now he seemed to be whispering . . . *two* thousand will not be enough.

In the end the revised plans drawn up by the architect

showed a sanctuary seating 2,300.

So began our great adventure. An architect's drawing, of course, is a far cry from an actual building in brick and glass and concrete. The banks all but laughed in our faces. As a humble independent church we were obviously at the very bottom of the credit-risk profile. Equally obviously, we had to have money. The check from Sears and the sale of the church at 4th and Grant together would barely pay for the foundation of the building we now proposed.

And so we did what churches all over the country were then doing with great success: we sold bonds.

Looking back I can see that in this undertaking in the mid-50s we did three things right—things which a decade later we neglected, to our peril. First, before we issued a single bond, members of our finance committee traveled around the country asking questions of churches with prior experience until we were satisfied that the system had benefits for all concerned. The organization issuing the bonds was able to borrow money at lower interest than banks were charging, while those buying them got a higher return than banks were paying. Above all, in every instance we knew of, the safety record for investors' money was impeccable.

Next, we were treading on such new territory that we asked God's help with every step. We sold our bonds first to ourselves, then we divided into teams and sold them to friends, neighbors, eventually to total strangers. What a stretching time it was! Many who had never sold anything in their lives found themselves daring to talk about Jesus to people they would otherwise never have approached.

Apparently what we were doing—the real estate transaction with Sears, the startlingly modern design of the proposed building, the fact that this unknown congregation proposed to erect by far the largest church in Denver—all this was more unusual that we realized, and the newspapers covered every development.

Ground breaking for the new building was on November 8, 1953. By spring it was clear that the project was costing more than we had bargained on.

And here the third principle entered in. By law you can raise only a certain percent of the value of a project by selling bonds, and we'd already reached that amount. Where was the additional money to come from? The papers got wind of our predicament. Was this upstart church that no one had ever heard of going to leave the city with a huge half-finished hulk on its hands?

Month by month we limped along, appealing to our radio audience, praying over every offering plate. In December, 1954, our general contractor came to see me. Jack Cys had a reputation as a fair and scrupulously honest businessman. "You folks haven't missed a payment yet," he said, standing in the door of my office at 4th and Grant, stamping the snow from his boots. "But from what I read in the paper you've hit the bottom of the barrel, and I figure we're $210,000 short of finished.

"Understand," he continued when he was seated, "I'm all for what you're trying to do. But I've seen too many of these religious outfits go broke and leave guys like me with workmen and suppliers to pay and no way to do it."

Thirty-five thousand dollars a month, he said, was the least he could keep operating on. As proof of our intentions he asked for six postdated checks, January to June 1955, for $35,000 each. "The first month a check doesn't clear, Mr. Blair, I'm taking my men off the job."

So that week we put the third principle into action: seek unity before any decision. Building committee, financial advisors, church board met in the sanctuary for an all-night prayer session. We did not get up off our knees until we sensed that oneness of spirit which had been the hallmark of this enterprise from its beginning. To every man and woman there the words came: "Issue the checks. I will supply."

Such confidence did this unanimity give me that I even risked a little humor when I reported our decision at the first service the following Sunday. "So we've given Mr. Cys those six checks," I concluded. "But you don't need to worry. I have a life insurance policy for more than that amount naming the church as beneficiary. If a check bounces I'll die of a heart attack and you can collect. I've even composed my tombstone." I turned around a large piece of composition board on which I had written:

Here lie the remains of Charles E. Blair.
He proved God does not answer prayer.

The congregation laughed and clapped and we were launched on the most eventful six months of our lives together. God was using a financial crisis, as he can use every crisis, to deepen our commitment, to purify our love. We saw that though we had prayed and worked and given, we had not yet given sacrificially. He showed us all kinds of things we could do without, at home, at work, to release the money to His service. At the end of each month there was money in the bank to cover that check, and every time it happened a different way. One month it was several large gifts from a few individuals. The next, with the deadline the following day and the account $6,040 short, He inspired us to empty our pockets and purses right there on Sunday morning. The total, at the end of the third service, was $6,045.35 . . .

By June the stunning edifice of brick, stone and stained glass stood complete on the corner of University and Alameda. June 26, 1955 was the dedication service. For the sense of continuity, we met for Sunday school first in the scattered quarters near the 4th and Grant building. Then we had a bumper-to-bumper automobile parade to the new building. The police gave us a motorcycle escort and we sang hymns all the way. Because of the newspaper coverage we arrived at University and Alameda to find the yet-unpaved parking lot filled with friends, sightseers, TV and radio trucks. Betty and I had had nightmares of an echoing three-quarters empty church, but thanks to the papers that huge sanctuary was filled to overflowing, 2,500 voices joining together as Betty took her seat at the organ and the white-robed choir filed into their tiers of seats.

Nor were those visions of an empty church ever realized.

The 2,300-seat figure which God had dropped into our incredulous minds proved warranted as Sunday after Sunday the big room remained packed to capacity. Within three years, in fact, people were again standing in the aisles and we added a second service. I believed our growth was due to the fact that we had determined never to spend more on ourselves than on others. Or perhaps it was the influence of the new TV show, or the daily radio broadcast. Whatever the reason we were considered a phenomenon in Colorado. "The man who can do no wrong," reporters began calling me.

And yet. . . . I remember the first time I discovered that not everything will yield to prayer and optimism. One spring day in 1961 I returned from church to find Betty, her mother and her sister Patty waiting for me in the living room.

"Mother's seen Dad!"

"Right on the street!"

"Here in Denver!"

When I could get them to speak one at a time I pieced together the story. That morning Mother Ruppert had taken the bus into downtown Denver—an unheard-of break in her stay-at-home existence. There on a busy midtown sidewalk she had suddenly found herself face to face with the husband she had not seen in 28 years. After a moment's stunned recognition, he had asked how she was, how his daughters were. He had been in the city several weeks, he said, working as a linotype operator at the *Denver Post*.

"Charles, Mother thinks he came here to be near us! He wouldn't say so, of course. He acted as if it were all just a coincidence. But he admitted he's been watching us on television."

Of course I telephoned him at the *Post* next morning and asked him to come have dinner with us. Betty and her mother were not sure he would show up and all day I half-hoped that he would not. What kind of relationship could I ever build with a man who had abandoned his wife and young daughters, to starve, as far as he ever bothered to find out. I also knew, however, that Betty had never stopped loving him, and that I had to try to love him too.

Patty and Don and their three children arrived an hour early at 5:30, and we sat nervously watching the clock while Mother and Betty and Vicki and Judy ran in and out of the kitchen and made a dozen adjustments in the already perfect table arrangements. Promptly at 6:30 a taxi stopped on the street outside and Virgil Ruppert stepped out. Muscular, athletic-looking, except for the unmistakable high color of the alcoholic, he was a strikingly handsome man.

But there was no trace of alcohol on his breath as he solemnly shook hands with each of us in turn, repeating the names of his grandchildren with a kind of wondering pleasure. The evening was less strained than I could have imagined possible as he regaled us with stories of the sports he loved. What had gone wrong, I asked myself all through the meal, in the life of this witty, intelligent, hard-working man, that he had reached the age of 56 homeless and hopeless? He talked freely about his drinking, repeating proudly that he'd never missed a night on the job, but admitting that alcohol had sabotaged everything else he touched. His second wife, he told us, had taken her own life many years before; he had no close friend anywhere on earth.

As we left the table and settled down in the living room it dawned on me that this was Virgil Ruppert's farewell. He told us he was dying; I was convinced, though he never said so, that he had come to Denver to see his wife and daughters before the end. We asked him to come live with us, but he wouldn't consider it. The most he would concede was to give us the name of the shabby downtown hotel where he was staying. Here Mother Ruppert or Betty or Patty would go to take him a hot casserole or do a little laundry for him in the cold-water basin. Most often they would find him on the bed, an empty half-pint bottle beside him on the floor. Again and again we repeated our invitation to come live with us; he always refused.

One day Betty arrived at the hotel to find a message at the desk. "Checked out yesterday, lady. He said to tell you he had some business to wrap up in San Francisco."

"To wrap up!" I grabbed eagerly at this straw. "Don't you see, honey, he's going to settle his affairs and come back here!"

But it was only hopeful thinking. One afternoon that fall, 1961, there was a call from the Denver Printers' Union. "We're looking for the daughter of Virgil Ruppert."

I knew from Betty's face what the news was: "He died this morning in the Kaiser Hospital in San Francisco. They need permission to release his body."

We got the hospital on the phone, then took the next plane out. He had been moved to a small funeral home. I had seen death from kidney failure many times, but never skin so discolored. The funeral was held there in the little parlor, attended by Betty, me and two men from the *Chronicle*, where he had last worked.

We buried him on a beautiful hillside south of the city. Virgil Ruppert, 56 years old, had maintained his independence to the end, determined to accept nothing on charity, not even the cost of his funeral. When they opened his locker at the paper they found, under an empty whiskey bottle, an insurance policy made out to Betty for $1,000. . . .

As the busy months followed I tried to block out this tragedy. There was a trip around the world—my third—to insure that our missionary dollars were being well spent. There were speaking trips across the country, and visits to Calvary Temple by men like E. Stanley Jones, J. Sidlow Baxter, Bishop Fulton J. Sheen, David Morken. It was an era of booming church growth, a time when success was in the air. The truth was that I and the men with whom I exchanged pulpits had become disdainful of failure. Failure was only lack of faith.

There was a derelict building not far from the church that aroused in me the same baffled emotions as the unfulfilled life of Virgil Ruppert. Two buildings, actually, standing side by side. They had been the grand dream of a local chiropractor, Dr. Leo Spears: eventually there were to have been four of the massive six-story structures, forming a great chiropractic center in the West. But Dr. Spears had died in 1956 when the first two buildings were only half complete, and there they stood, starting to crumble now, an eyesore to the community. Those buildings, like my father-in-law's death, were an offense to me. There was very little space in my theology for unrealized dreams.

Success crowned our personal lives, too, when in 1963 we moved into a spacious new home. We'd been in the little house on Vine Street nearly 14 years. Vicki and Judy, teenagers now, needed separate rooms and Mother Ruppert could use a little independence. Betty proposed therefore to do her own contracting once again. Once more she was on the phone at all hours with plumbers, roofers, gravel and cement suppliers.

"The builder thinks I'm a widow," she complained one night. "He never lays eyes on you."

Indeed, I hardly saw my own family anymore, with committee meetings every night of the week when I was not off traveling. But with or without my assistance the house was completed. Betty and Mother and the girls made the move one weekend while I was speaking in New York. It was in a brand new subdivision on the south side of the city, on a street to which the developer had given the hopeful name of Happy Canyon. Out the back window we could see the eastern slope of the Rockies all the way from Pike's Peak to Mount Evans. Mother Ruppert, we teasingly reminded her, was back in the basement—but this time it was a sunny above-ground room with a private entrance and its own bath.

It was our dream house indeed, and my favorite spot in it was our bedroom. In one corner was the green overstuffed chair which Betty used for her prayer time. Books were piled around it; they overflowed our night tables, they filled the double headboard that ran behind the twin beds.

And it was in this comfortable cluttered room in the winter of 1964, the year after we moved to Happy Canyon, that I had the dream that was to change our lives.

13

In the dream I stood on a landscaped lawn outside a pair of handsome six-story buildings, watching people stream in and out of the canopied entryways.

That was all.

And yet, as I dreamed, there seemed to be some special urgency about what I was seeing. What could be so significant about these imaginary edifices? There were no such actual buildings—none I was familiar with anyway.

And then, still in the dream, I recognized them. It was that abandoned medical center of Dr. Spears! In reality, only concrete shells. And yet in the dream I was seeing them complete, occupied, in use.

The shock of recognition woke me up. For perhaps an hour I struggled to get back to sleep, but the strange, vivid dream stayed with me. I tossed from side to side until Betty's sleepy voice came from her own bed.

"What's the matter, Charles?"

"Nothing. A dream I can't seem to get rid of."

"Tell me in the morning."

But I couldn't get back to sleep and so, of course, neither could Betty: "Oh all right, Charles. Tell me now."

When I finished, she was silent so long I wondered if she had fallen asleep. "I can't imagine either," she said at last, "why you should dream of those particular buildings. They can't have anything to do with us."

I rolled over, turning my back to her. It seemed to me, there in the dark, that Betty of late was having difficulty catching the Spirit's spark. She seemed to be suggesting more and more often that it was time to center down, to simplify.

"That's one of the differences between men and women," I said to myself. "We men are just natural builders."

One day, a couple of weeks after that inexplicable dream, my secretary, Joan Bjork, buzzed to remind me that I was scheduled to go for a drive that afternoon with one of the men from church. Lex Dolton was a bit mysterious as we braved the cold and headed along East Colfax. He kept hinting that this was more than just a casual spin. "There's a building I want you to see, Pastor," he confessed at last. "I drove past it the other day and found myself wondering if the church could do something with it."

At once I recalled my dream. Lex was driving straight toward the site of those six-story concrete skeletons. My heart began to race as we turned off Colfax.

"Lex," I said, "I had a dream the other night. I dreamed about that old chiropractic center. You know—the eyesore on 8th and Ivy? Only in my dream the buildings were finished."

Lex turned to stare. "Pastor, that's incredible! That's the very place we're headed!"

We finished the trip in silence. Lex turned in to the rubble-strewn lot and turned off the motor. Debris lay everywhere. Incomplete plumbing dangled from the bare walls, exactly as workmen had left them when they abandoned the project eight years earlier. "Want to walk around?" Lex asked.

So we got out of the warm automobile and picked our way over frozen puddles and boards sticking out of the ground. I was shivering, whether from cold or excitement I couldn't tell. I was remembering those early days in Denver, after my trip to Memphis to visit Dr. Lee, when I would make the rounds of city hospitals. These buildings, completed, staffed with Christian doctors and nurses, could become such a facility—with the enormous difference that everyone on the staff, from admissions clerks to janitors, would be as concerned for the patient's spiritual health as for his physical condition.

Not just any patient, the thoughts raced on. Here we could bring the elderly and the handicapped, the men and women who never had a visitor, the ones who, in other institutions, were relegated to cheerless corners in back wards. Here we'd surround them with the loving concern of our large and committed congregation. . . .

Lex clambered at my side across fallen chunks of concrete on what had been intended as the ground floor. He must have known that an enormous vision was forming itself in my mind because he was very quiet.

"Lex," I burst out, "what have we got to lose? Let's find out if this place is for sale."

"My thought exactly!" Lex said. "The Spears brothers' offices are right over there." He pointed through the open side of the building toward a sprawling, brown-brick clinic on the adjacent block.

We got back into Lex's automobile, blowing on our fingers, and drove to the front entrance of the Spears Chiropractic Clinic. Dr. Dan Spears and Dr. Howard Spears—nephews of the Leo Spears who had begun the abandoned complex next door—both happened to be in.

Lex and I stepped behind the white-frocked nurse into a small consulting room where Dr. Dan and Dr. Howard greeted us cordially. Their office—as their clinic—was not glamorous, but spoke of men who took on all clients regardless of their ability to pay.

"Always good to see you, Pastor," Dr. Dan said. I had met him earlier at his uncle's funeral. He indicated two chairs and the four of us sat down. Somewhat embarrassed, I told the brothers about my dream.

"When was this, Pastor?" Dr. Howard Spears asked.

"About two weeks ago."

"Incredible!" both men said at once. That was the very time, they told us, that they had decided to sell the uncompleted center. "We sat right here in this office," Dr. Dan said, "and agreed that we were never going to do a thing with those buildings."

"And," put in Dr. Howard, "you won't believe what we also said. 'Do you think Charles Blair would be interested?' But we didn't call you because we figured you were too busy already to take on a project of this size."

Well, I walked out of that clinic a very excited man. I could hardly wait to tell Betty. Surely she too would see the unmistakable hand of God in these coincidences.

But when that night, in the seclusion of our bedroom, I related the day's experiences, she once again failed to catch the vision. She was sitting in her green overstuffed chair, the book she had been reading open in her lap.

"It seems to me, Charles, that you're already stretched to the breaking point. Where will you find time to listen to God when you're already working 26 hours a day?"

It was a bucket of cold water thrown on the fire of my excitement, and I came up sputtering. "How long do you have to listen, when the need's in front of your nose? Aren't we told to take care of the widows and orphans?"

How long do you have to listen . . . So often, in the years ahead, I was to wish I had heeded my own question! *As long as necessary,* I should have answered, *to be absolutely certain it is His voice you hear.*

"No one argues with the need, dear," Betty was saying gently. "The question is whether it has our name on it. Do you remember, Charles, when you were so sure we were to go to Manila? And what Mr. Perkin said? 'It isn't the need we see around us; it's finding God's will for each life.' "

"He showed me His will in that dream," I insisted. "Confirmed by Lex this afternoon. The Spears brothers too—my name popped right into their heads."

Still . . . Betty was right, of course. Guidance couldn't be checked out too carefully. "I'll submit it to the church board before doing anything," I assured her.

And submit it I did. In February, 1965, I laid before the 50-man board of Calvary Temple the possibility of the church's acquiring the abandoned Spears complex. But I did so with an enthusiasm that made it hard to disagree. When I'd asked the church to pray about our call to Manila, 15 years before, I'd been genuinely confused about my guidance. This time I was convinced that I had heard God's voice. After all, I was a lot more experienced. I was no longer a struggling young preacher, but pastor of the largest church in Denver. A man with—God help him!—a reputation for success.

Conversations with various hospital administrators had confirmed my own impressions: a nursing facility for the aged and handicapped was needed in the city. I came to the board meeting armed with sheets of statistics. "God has an answer to this human suffering," I remember saying, "and we at Calvary Temple are called to be part of it."

Not surprisingly, there was little debate. One man disagreed to the point of resigning. Maybe no one else felt this way. Maybe many did. The point is, my own excitement about the project prevented me from finding out.

In March, 1965, after further talks with the Spears brothers, and with professionals in the health-care field, I held a press conference at the Continental Denver to announce our new adventure. With a down payment of one dollar, a non-profit corporation called Life Center, Inc., had purchased the old Spears Chiropractic Hospital. The purchase price represented the actual cash Leo Spears had put into the land and buildings more than eight years ago, $1,250,000.

We were going to spend an additional six million to complete and renovate the derelict buildings. They would become one of the first Christian medical centers in the world to specialize in geriatric problems. We were going to hire the very best administrators and medical personnel we could find, Christian men and women who would treat the whole person, not separating body from mind and spirit. Control of Life

Center would be in the hands of an 11-man board consisting of three medical men, three clergymen, and five laymen. Life Center would be an outreach of Calvary Temple, yet totally separate from the church administratively and financially. We were answering a need in our community, taking care of the elderly and the infirm with the outstretched hands of Jesus.

"Where will the money for all this come from?" one reporter asked.

"Fund raising," I answered with supreme assurance. "Plus, of course a little borrowing to get started."

On my way home I thought about that confident answer. But surely in this case confidence was justified? For years we had mixed fund raising and borrowing at Calvary Temple, always paying back our debts on time or ahead of schedule. Our impeccable financial record was, I thought, one of our great strengths.

What I did not know then was that a Christian is in greatest danger not at his weak points but at his strong ones. Where we are strong we are also off guard. Where we are confident we are not often enough on our knees.

14

Just as I expected, over the next several months our congregations at Calvary and our radio and TV audiences responded with characteristic selflessness to fund raising appeals for Life Center. And this at a time when other drives of ours were underway. We purchased 42 acres of land across Alameda, known locally as "the Polo Grounds," for the school we proposed to build. We moved into nearby houses as we outgrew our central building. Already we were planning an extension to our only-four-year-old Sunday school wing, and we discussed an immense new sanctuary, double the size of our present auditorium, to ease the crowding at our three Sunday services.

So much was going on that I was startled to realize, driving out Colfax one February morning in 1966, that over a year had passed since Lex Dolton and I took that ride. The two skeleton buildings stood exactly as we had seen them. Crumbling a little more at the edges, perhaps, the rust around the unconnected pipe fittings a little more evident.

Back in my office I got our financial secretary to dig out the figures on Life Center. My impression was correct: we'd spent a lot of money—over $100,000 in fact—with nothing whatever to show for it. Of course, the secretary reminded me, buying the property for one dollar left the entire purchase price of one-and-a-quarter million in the form of a mortgage. Interest alone on that amount was more than $100,000 a year, and then there were lawyers' and accountants' fees, building-use and stress studies, studies on the types and amounts of medical service required—all before the first load of cement could be poured.

And, of course, until the buildings were completed and occupied not a penny of these expenses could be recouped. Clearly the thing to do was to get on with the construction. And contributions from our people, generous as they were, barely kept pace with our interest payments. A construction loan seemed the obvious answer. "A little borrowing," I'd told the reporter, "to get started." And so, accompanied by businessmen from our congregation, I began calling on loan officers at banks in the Denver area.

We quickly discovered that banks weren't interested. "It isn't that your credit is bad, gentlemen," one vice-president explained. "Your rating is excellent. It's your expertise that worries us. Building and managing medical centers requires a lifetime of experience and you have none at all. I know you're planning to hire the expertise but, believe me, it's a full-time job *supervising supervisors.* Who'll be the responsible party?"

Well—I would. With knowledgeable people running things, that shouldn't take a great deal of time, I said to myself, driving back to the office that April morning.

I suppose the stalemate we faced at the banks, plus the fact that as I traveled about the country I saw other pastors going into monumental building programs, set me up for a visit to Chicago one day in the late fall of 1966, almost two years after Lex and I had driven out to 8th and Ivy.

Seven pastors, each with a thriving church and each with a popular television ministry, met in a suite of rooms at the fashionable Beachwater Hotel. Flowers and fruit arrived from the management, room service brought hot coffee in a silver urn.

When I described the opportunity that had been presented to us in Denver in the form of Life Center, and the problems we faced getting a bank loan, there was a unanimous response.

"That's not the way it's done, Charles!" Nobody, it seemed, ("nobody with our kind of public exposure") depended on banks to get a major project going. "Banks have no daring. The people—that's our base of support."

Of course, you couldn't ask people just to give, give, give. "You *borrow* from the public, Charles. Then as soon as your project starts producing income you repay them. We've raised hundreds of thousands of dollars this way."

"Hundreds of thousands?" another man echoed scornfully. "Millions!"

Did I detect a spirit of competitiveness along with the mutual love and respect in that Chicago hotel room? Many of us, I knew, came from the same depression-haunted childhoods. With this background of poverty, was there an undue emphasis on impressive figures and statistics?

Yet it sounded so logical, borrowing money this way. We'd been doing it for years, in fact, at Calvary Temple, and no one had ever failed to receive full interest or get all of his money back. So it was that I came back to Denver from Chicago ready to put a new emphasis on borrowing.

I had in mind just the man to head up this effort, too. Wendell Nance. An enthusiastic, vital man in his mid-40s, Wendell had twice been the featured speaker during stewardship missions at Calvary. Wendell never walked, he galloped. He seemed to have an ideal balance between depending on God and depending on hard work. I intended to get in touch with Wendell right away, but I didn't have a chance. Wendell called me, instead, long distance.

"I'm in Kansas City, Pastor," Wendell said, "and I was wondering if you could spare an hour. I'm at a fork in the road and I need advice." Again, that incredible confirmation which seemed to accompany every phase of this project!

And so Wendell galloped in, charming everyone with his

energy and optimism. Over the next few weeks he met with the elders and top business people at church. Did any of us ask ourselves if this whole approach was out of line with God's will? I know that I did not. Any cautionary notes, it seemed to me, came from people who were not bold enough in their faith.

In January, 1967, Wendell officially joined us as the man who would find the money, at last, to get this project underway. Ironically this was also the date we had originally projected for the Grand Opening of Life Center. The buildings stood exactly as Lex and I had seen them, yet by now we had spent nearly a quarter of a million dollars in interest and research costs.

Wendell's first job, before we could solicit investments, was to write a prospectus which then had to be submitted to the Securities and Exchange Commission.

"What's a prospectus, Mr. Nance?" 19-year-old Judy asked one evening. We were seated around the dinner table at our home on Happy Canyon Drive.

"A prospectus," Wendell answered, "is a document telling an investor what the *prospects* are for his investment. What the purpose of the bond issue is. Who the officers and directors are. A little resume of their lives and experience. It has to show the cost of selling the bonds themselves and what percentage of the overall costs that will represent. It discloses the salaries of the officers. That kind of thing. The investor has to know exactly what he is getting into."

"Then the SEC approves?" I asked, not knowing much more than Judy how these things went. Until recently, under Colorado law, churches selling securities had not been required to have prospectuses.

"The SEC never actually approves in so many words. They will tell you that your prospectus meets their guidelines, but that's all. They can *disapprove,* but they don't like to put their seal on a project."

"And if they disapprove?" Judy asked.

"I don't see why they should," said Wendell. "Everything

is extremely straightforward. And if there are problems," he added with the buoyancy I loved, "well, obstacles are created so that we can overcome them, right?"

Our prospectus showed four buildings, eventually, as in Leo Spears' original design. Initially, however, we intended to complete only the first two and get them into operation before taking on further expense. The new goal for the opening of Towers One and Two was 1970. It would take that long to design the fine plant we had in mind, raise the money, secure the staff.

I was glad we'd allowed so much time as snags developed over building permits, foundation requirements, specifications for the curtain walls, parking space. All these delays occurred at a time when construction costs were skyrocketing. It began to look as though—whenever we finally began work—the six million we had originally projected would fall considerably short.

Except for these aggravations over Life Center, however, things couldn't have been going better. Not only at church, but at home too. In January, 1967, Vicki married a young soldier, Jack Moore, with whom she'd sung in the church choir. Jack was the son of missionaries, which pleased Betty and me especially. Then in June, 1968, Judy married Roger Anderson, another "choir romance," a boy we'd known and liked for years, with a promising career as a salesman. With two sons-in-law, Betty and I felt that we had the family we'd always wanted. This was especially true with the birth of our first grandchild, Marrles Moore, in April, 1969. I looked forward to going fishing and hunting with Marrles as I already did with Roger and Jack.

Things were going well in other areas too. The radio ministry that Betty and I had started 20 years earlier was thriving. Our televised service at Calvary Temple was viewed by 100,000 each week. At our lawyers' suggestion we formed a non-profit corporation, the Charles E. Blair Foundation, to expand our TV outreach and to receive funds from the television audience for Life Center. In July, 1969, *Decision* magazine carried an article about us as part of their "Great Churches" series. It was hard to keep from feeling proud at their summary of our growth. Especially in the area of giving: we had donated more than $2,000,000 over the years to missions and were currently helping to support 85 missionary families around the world. At home we had eight pastors and 45 employees, nine choirs and three choral groups.

In 1969, too, construction at last got started on the two long-abandoned towers at 8th and Ivy. Thanks to Wendell Nance and the hard-working group of bond salesmen he had recruited, it began to look as though Life Center would meet its projected opening date of 1970 after all. It was great to see the tall cranes in place, cement trucks bumping over the ground, workmen clambering about the scaffolding.

One other good thing happened to us in 1969. At least it seemed like a good thing at the time. . . .

"The Castle" was the local nickname given to a house built 35 years earlier on Cedar Street, down the block from the church. The name came from the fact that the Tudor-style house, set on two acres of landscaped perfection, had a hexagonal tower rising above the entry. One day a friend in real estate came to see me. Did I know that the owners of the Castle intended to sell? Would Calvary Temple be interested? It was true that the church had bought two other houses in the neighborhood, one to use as a youth center, the other to house one of our pastors and his family. But the Castle! The place was a mansion.

My friend persisted. Surely I'd heard the rumor that the area was to be rezoned for high-rise apartments? I hadn't. But that was a consideration indeed. Traffic congestion here on Sunday morning was already horrendous. Add a lot of apartment buildings. . . .

In the end, a church committee was set up to look into it.

One sweltering afternoon in July, 1970, I came into my office to find a message from Wendell Nance. He wanted to see me with some good news.

I had to laugh. That was so like Wendell. I just could not

imagine Mr. Enthusiasm wanting to see me with bad news. Wendell had certainly been the right man for the job. It was hard to believe that he had been working on the Life Center project for three-and-a-half years now. Recently, Wendell had moved into an office at the building site and I did not see him as often as I used to. I missed his ebullient personality and his contagious optimism. If a mountain of difficulties loomed ahead, Wendell only shrugged. "That's no hill at all for a real climber!" he'd say.

I looked up to see Wendell himself standing in the doorway. For the first time I noticed that his hair, solid black when he came with us, was showing traces of grey.

"Wendell, it's really good to see you! How do you like your new offices?" When he moved he had transferred with him his entire staff—attorneys, secretaries, fund raisers, junior administrators. He had more room now but our communication suffered.

"They're the best, Pastor! The best. And do I have great news about the grand opening!" I waved Wendell toward the sofa.

"First," he said, "the Evangelical Lutheran Good Samaritan Society has signed." That *was* good news. We had been interviewing nursing home managers, and quickly discovered that the best firms were choosy. They wouldn't accept all clients, only those whose facilities met the highest standards. The Good Samaritans had been our first choice to manage Life Center; we considered them the very best in the field.

"Not only that," Wendell went on, "but the October 25 dedication is going to be a tremendous occasion! Senator Allott has agreed to come, so has the governor and Mayor McNichols. The color guard from the Air Force Academy is going to present the colors. I've set up TV and radio coverage. With this kind of sponsorship, Pastor, we shouldn't have any trouble raising the five million we still need."

Sunday, October 25, 1970, was bright and cold. As Betty and Mother Ruppert and I drove out to Life Center I recalled the day, nearly six years earlier, when Lex Dolton and I had followed this same route to gaze at a pair of concrete skeletons. Today the two buildings rose finished and gleaming behind the ribbon-dressed bandstand, exactly as I had seen them in my dream.

The exteriors, that is, were finished; beneath the exterior skin only Tower One was actually ready to receive patients. It had cost as much to complete and equip that single building as the original estimate for the two of them. But, as Wendell said, selling bonds in a "going concern"—and one that was having the kind of send-off we were seeing today—should be no problem.

A strange, very slight shadow was cast over the day during Senator Allott's speech. I'm sure I was the only one to notice it, but the shadow was there nonetheless. "The men and women who have made this center a reality," the senator said, "have given a dramatic demonstration that determined men and women can change the world through their own efforts."

Through their own efforts. The phrase, meant as a tribute to the hard work of many, rang warningly in my ears. Were we really doing all this *through our own efforts?*

If so, our troubles weren't behind us at all.

The worrisome thought passed in a flurry of ribbon cutting. As the red, white, and blue streamers fluttered to the ground there was a surge up the broad steps and into the warm building.

The great mirrored lobby with its splashing fountain and beautiful planting drew compliments. But most admired were the four model rooms on display, one done in Early American style, one in French Provincial, one in Mediterranean, one in Oriental. Each had color TV, individual air conditioning, private bath. All were in stunning contrast to the cheerless rooms I still visited each week in my rounds of shut-ins, and my own high point of the day came when I overheard a lady comment.

"I'm so glad my mother has a place like this to come to!"

On Tuesday our first patient, Jane Laybourn, a young polio victim, was admitted, followed by two elderly sisters and a 93-year-old man who had lost both hearing and sight. Now at last people at Calvary Temple could take part in Life Center in other ways than passing a hat. Residents' rooms were never without fresh flowers or a bowl of fruit; as the Center's population grew, church groups took charge of a transportation program and a daily worship service.

Life Center was truly so full of life, so grounded in prayer and caring, that at first I tended to be impatient with what seemed to me the constant nagging of our financial people. Less than three months after our grand opening, both our in-house attorney, Warren Charles, and our church accountant, Ralph Bartsch, warned in separate memos that our annual audit, in 1970, showed Life Center operating at an enormous loss.

Well, we'd never expected to make a profit on the project. At long last the Center was fulfilling its purpose, wasn't it? Caring for the crippled and the elderly, obeying God's commandment to love our neighbor. Where was their faith?

Faith, Warren and Ralph answered patiently, did not excuse us from our obligations to the Securities and Exchange Commission. Once we *borrowed* that first penny from the public, they explained, (as opposed to money raised through gifts, which did not have to be paid back) we had become subject to all the various laws intended to safeguard the lender. One of these laws, Warren stressed, was that the *assets* of the entity issuing the bonds—whether it was an oil company or a car manufacturer or a church—had to exceed by a stated margin its *liabilities*.

But here even the experts ceased to agree. What were the assets of Life Center? Net worth, apparently, could vary greatly, depending on accounting procedure. Should we choose, for example, rapid or slow depreciation of buildings and equipment? Were Life Center's land and buildings valued at what we paid for them, or what they could be sold for? Then there was the issue of start-up expenses—the years of research, all the pre-operational expenses that were not represented by tangible physical objects. Were they a part of our assets or were they not? If you did not, for instance, include start-up costs for *Gone with the Wind,* the value of the film before distribution was the price of the celluloid. Yet one outside accountant totaling our assets put our start-up costs as "without value."

Tied in with all this was the requirement of "full disclosure" of Life Center's financial picture to potential investors. Here not only accounting procedures were in question but public psychology. I might be a neophyte where it came to business, but where human nature was concerned I had plenty of experience. And that experience convinced me: "nothing succeeds like success."

My bleak childhood had persuaded me that the opposite was true too: nothing fails like failure. The reporters who labeled me *the man who can do no wrong* didn't know how damning their observation was. I could *not* be wrong; I did not dare to fail. Success, it seemed to me, depended above all on *appearing* successful, like Wichita *Eagle* salesmen who might stay in quarter-a-night sleeping rooms, but wore suits and fresh-shined shoes when they rang customers' doorbells.

And how we needed that aura of success right now, when raising money was suddenly critical. Meeting the day-to-day operating expenses of Tower One, completing the interior of Tower Two, paying for construction recently begun on Towers Three and Four, meeting interest payments on the money we had borrowed up to now—all of this was adding up to far more than we had bargained for.

The key I felt was the sales team Wendell had recruited: eager, energetic men who had caught the vision of Life Center and were fanning out across the country inspiring people with their own excitement. Of course it cost money to do this. There were glossy printings and large mailings, airplane tickets and phone bills, salesmen's salaries and expense accounts. A successful salesman after all couldn't wear a frayed collar or drive a beat-up old car. Above all, he could not represent our bonds as risky. There *was* no risk to anyone putting money into Life Center, of that I was absolutely convinced. Not only would the Center eventually have enough residents to make it financially viable—once all four towers were completed—but Life Center bonds were backed by the good name and reputation of Calvary Temple itself.

And so, since investors were certain to get their money back, with interest, and since anyhow the money men were in disagreement about the financial picture, we encouraged the salesmen to present the bonds in the brightest possible light. . . .

In May, 1971, seven months after the grand opening of Life Center, the decision was made by the church to go ahead and purchase the Castle. It would be a good long-term investment, we felt; meanwhile it could be put to good use by our minister of music.

In every way 1971 was the best year Calvary Temple had ever known. That summer we started production on the television series that was my newest dream. Titled "Better World," the programs illustrated the progress, health and joy which I passionately believed were God's will for each of us. In pursuit of my theme I spent time with the historian Arnold Toynbee in his London apartment, visited a kibbutz with David ben-Gurion, interviewed Dr. Jonas Salk, who developed the polio vaccine, and Dr. Roger Bannister, who broke the four-minute mile.

Negatives were thus the last thing on my mind when in January, 1972, Joan Bjork came into my office wearing a frown. "Pastor, I think you'd better look at this."

I glanced up from the letters I was signing. With the travel I was doing, just keeping up with correspondence was hard. "What is it, Joan?"

"The latest report from the department of development."

Wendell's department of development! I smiled, remembering the Christmas party at Life Center just last month. Gifts for each of the 250 residents, the colorful packages heaped beneath the huge tree in the lobby; a singing group from church; Jane Laybourn, first person to call the Center home, leading a word game from her wheelchair.

Joan, however, was not smiling. Something in her manner made me push the stack of letters to one side and pick up the sheets of figures she laid in front of me. I spent the better part of an hour going over charts and reports, then got Wendell Nance on the telephone.

Wendell, I noticed when he arrived, was continuing to grey. Had five years working with us done this to him? I said I was worried about the staggering expenses in the department of development. Was there any way we could cut back?

"Well, Charles," Wendell said, taking off his glasses and cleaning them, "here is the problem we're up against. . . ."

Wendell then reviewed for me the Life Center situation. Things had been "tumbling," he said (I remember being struck by his choice of words) in a beautiful way toward realizing our objectives. In the first two towers, 255 beds were now occupied; another 155 would be available by the end of the month. Couple this with plans for completing further floors of Tower Two as retirement residences for people who did not require intensive nursing, and we would, under normal circumstances, be in very good shape.

"But, Pastor, don't forget that these are not normal times. The whole country is in a terrible money squeeze." Giving, nationwide, was down by 40%. Our best hope, Wendell felt, was to speed up the program for the completion of Towers Three and Four. Push on through! With all four buildings operating we'd have no trouble converting the expensive bonds into a low-cost conventional loan from an insurance company.

"So that's the strategy," Wendell said. "But it does mean putting an all-out effort into selling bonds this upcoming year."

Which, I could see, was all by way of saying that although we were spending a great deal of money to raise money, the solution was to spend still more. . . .

Hindsight vision is always 20-20. I can see now what I should have done. I should have listened, then said, "I agree, Wendell, that we want to attract the highest caliber salesman and give him the tools to do the job. But what's a reasonable salary for this job? Do we need a whole fleet of cars? Can we defend every single employee on the payroll? For everyone's sake, let's call in an unbiased outside firm to give us a cost-efficiency check."

I should have insisted on a better balance between borrowing and our customary means of raising money through donations. With giving off, in the 70s, that automatically would have meant slowing down. Even stopping for a while. We'd get our conventional loan on the two completed buildings and wait until we had built up a solid cash position with income from these first two towers before putting another nail into the second two.

Above all, I should have recognized the danger of my own emotional commitment to those four finished towers. I should have gotten down on my knees, then submitted my guidance to praying men and women for confirmation or denial.

That's what I should have done.

What I did do was return home convinced by logic that it was proper to push ahead, "believing." That night I told Betty only the bright spots of my talk with Wendell. "We've claimed all four towers, complete, as soon as possible! It won't be easy—but no territory is won for the Lord without a battle."

Betty said nothing at all.

Our sessions with the SEC resumed, this time trying to get a new prospectus passed for Towers Three and Four. We had long since met the requirements on the first prospectus, dated June 1, 1970, for Towers One and Two. At the end of January I took off on another missionary trip to the Far East, confident that the new prospectus was only a matter of time. Surely, with new residents moving in every day, there could be no grounds for disapproval.

I got back on February 16, 1972, and bounded up the side steps to the church, happy to be home. My desk was piled high with correspondence which Joan had arranged according to content: requests for money, invitations to speak, people with personal problems seeking counsel. I glanced through the accumulation while taking off my overcoat. One small pile, I saw, was labelled "Priority." Perhaps, Joan suggested, I'd want to look at these right away?

I sat down at the desk and thumbed through the priority letters. There were several notes from Wendell, one from our staff attorney Warren Charles, and one from Garth Grissom, a personal friend and member of a prestigious Denver law firm who often worked with Warren on church legal affairs. From the outer office I heard Joan asking a staffer to come back in a little while because I was taking care of "urgent business." Urgent?

A little less casually, now, I started to read. The memos from Wendell were so typical of him. I chuckled, feeling very affectionate. Excitement was running high at Life Center, he wrote. Things were "popping" there. The floors at Tower Two to be used as retirement residences had model apartments furnished now, ready for inspection. The new Christian counseling facility would begin functioning in two weeks. Wendell even managed to make bad news palatable. We were presently operating at a deficit at Life Center, but Wendell reported that the Phoenix Mutual Insurance Company was so impressed with our future prospects that they were definitely going to grant us a huge loan.

"I have a 'click' in my heart," wrote Wendell, "that we are on the right track."

Garth Grissom's letter was less pleasant reading. In it he summarized our position. The first two towers—one still only partially complete on the inside—had already cost us some $10,000,000. About half of this money had been raised through the sale of secured bonds. Much of the balance, however, was financed through the sale of *unsecured* notes, called "time payment certificates." It was the growing number of these unsecured obligations that bothered Garth, because the chief selling feature, stressed by our salesmen, was that these were repayable at any time, simply at the request of the certificate holder.

"If for any reason there should be a wholesale tendering of the time payment certificates," Garth wrote, "Life Center simply could not meet its obligations. . . ."

Well—but, why should great numbers of people suddenly decide to ask for their money? We'd used time payment certificates several times in the past, raising money for projects at church, and never had a problem. I liked to tell people that such certificates, based only on people's confidence in Calvary Temple's word, were as secure as any collateral-backed bond in the world. When someone wanted his money we simply resold his certificate to the next applicant in line. There were always more people eager to invest in Calvary Temple projects than we had notes to sell. There always would be. Wouldn't there?

I turned uneasily to the last letter. It was from our in-house attorney, Warren Charles. And it went even further than Garth's. Warren spoke of the "dire" financial condition of Life Center, and of the fact that we were under obligation to warn potential investors about this condition. Such disclosure is required by law, Warren reminded me. Unless we did that, and until we got a positive response from the SEC on our prospectus for Towers Three and Four, we should immediately stop selling securities for the Center.

Stop selling? But . . . that would mean stopping construction! The two unfinished towers bristled with scaffolding and exposed air conditioning conduits. Future access roads and parking lots were muddy fields, the site of the triple fountain and reflecting pools mere holes in the ground. To stop now would demoralize residents and staff and neighbors.

And contributors. Who would want to put his money into a

project that had bogged down—into one that did not spell success?

Still, the letters from Garth and Warren left little alternative. With as heavy a heart as I'd known for years, I picked up the phone and told Wendell that his development team, deployed in a dozen cities across the country, must halt all sales of Life Center securities.

"But only for a while, Wendell," I assured him. "Only until our income picture improves enough to satisfy the SEC."

On March 2, 1972, two weeks after I had made this decision, we had a letter from a Mr. Joseph Krys of the SEC requesting further clarification of our finances. "They're moving at last on our request!" I exulted. Wendell spent a week preparing a detailed reply. He submitted our last financial statement, dated the previous September, and enclosed the prospectus which we had used for the sale of securities to finance Towers One and Two. Wendell acknowledged that our operating statements showed substantial losses, but stressed that such losses were expected until more rooms were completed and occupied. Once that happened, we were confident that the picture would get better. He promised a new prospectus.

I liked his answer and hoped it would satisfy the SEC.

Two days later I flew to New York to put the voice-over sound track onto a segment of our Better World television series. It was difficult, maintaining the enthusiasm which the very positive script demanded, knowing that one vision for a "better world" was at this moment snarled in financial woes and governmental red tape.

At the close of one recording session a secretary told me that I'd received a call from Denver. "A Mr. Garth Grissom. He wants you to call him back."

I returned the call from a private lounge, the sounds of Madison Avenue, seven stories below, drifting faintly into the room. Something out of the ordinary must have come up—Garth would never have telephoned me at the studio on a routine matter.

"Garth? Charles. Hope everything back there is fine."

"As a matter of fact, Pastor, things are not fine. We have another letter from Joseph Krys."

"From the SEC? Your voice tells me it's bad news."

"It is, Charles." The letter was in answer to Wendell's optimistic-sounding correspondence of March 10, 1972. It said that in view of the fact that our earlier prospectus of June 1, 1970, was nearly two years out of date and did not reflect the worsening financial condition of Life Center, our substantial operating losses and the total amount of the first mortgage bonds, therefore, ". . . it is suggested that you terminate all further sales of those securities."

"But we've done that, Garth."

"I know. Now we come to the bad news."

What could be worse, I wondered.

"The SEC is taking the position that Life Center is operating a Ponzi scheme."

"Come again, Garth?"

"Ponzi. It was a famous legal case back in Boston. A fellow by the name of Ponzi sold a lot of securities in a project that wasn't making money. When interest was due he simply sold more securities, and used that money to pay the earlier lenders. When *that* interest came due, he sold further securities, and so on. The courts found this illegal. Well, let me read you from Mr. Krys' letter. 'The operation of a Ponzi scheme violates the antifraud provisions of the federal securities laws.' "

"Did you say *fraud*, Garth?"

"I didn't say it, Pastor. That's the SEC's word."

Back in Denver I faced a dispirited staff at the Department of Development, who felt that their work had been aborted.

"Our prospects are so good," one salesman, called back from Atlanta, said. "I thought that's what the word 'prospectus' meant—looking ahead. Tomorrow looks very good."

"Phoenix Mutual thinks so," said Wendell. It was true that there were two outside opinions, now, regarding our situation. And they were exact opposites, depending on whether they were reached from a forward-looking or a backward-looking viewpoint. Phoenix Mutual, seeking a safe loan, believed that our tomorrow was healthy; the SEC, looking back over the money we had already spent, believed that we were unhealthy.

In any event we now had no choice but to refrain from selling and shift our emphasis altogether to seeking donations. In a curious way I was glad. I was more experienced in this area, and it was less subject to abuse. In recent months some of our representatives had undoubtedly let their enthusiasm run away with their judgment. Hearing about the nine percent interest our bonds paid, one lady had taken her life savings of $35,000 from the bank. Our salesman urged her to hold back $10,000 for emergencies. But she went ahead: "If you can't trust the church," she told him, "who can you trust!" Another man was so excited about our work that he wanted to take out a loan on his car to lend us the money. When I heard about it I passed word to our staff that we did not want that kind of excess. But in most cases it was already too late.

15

The Phoenix Mutual loan went through on April 7, 1972. Buoyed by this show of confidence, we submitted a new prospectus proposal to the SEC for Towers Three and Four. Surely they would approve now. But summer came and went with no word. And in fact the Phoenix Mutual loan had a backfire effect on donations. People felt that we were adequately financed now, and gift-giving slowed way down. Barely enough came in to keep a token crew at work on the new buildings.

Meanwhile, in spite of legal and financial problems, all of us acquainted with the actual flesh-and-blood people living in the first two towers at 8th and Ivy remained convinced as ever that Life Center was an important place, a needed place, a place God Himself had willed into existence. Walking the cheerful corridors gave me the same joy I had felt visiting hospitals in my early years in Denver—only many times more so. Here each room was like the bedroom in a private home, with curtains at the windows, matching bedspreads, colorful wallpaper. The dining room, the chapel, the library, the counseling rooms, glowed with caring. Here staffers prayed for residents, as well as serving them; here those with tragedies too big to handle alone found help.

I remember one evening arriving on the maximum care wing to learn that a new patient had been admitted that day. John Folks was a 17-year-old orphan who for most of his life had been shunted from one foster parent to another. One afternoon he was standing on the porch of a neighbor's house when a bullet severed his spinal cord.

"The police think that the gun was probably not aimed at John at all," the nurse said to me. "He simply got in the way."

We stopped in front of John's room. "What's the outlook?" I asked in a whisper.

"He can move his head, nothing else."

"Does he know he won't get better?"

The nurse took a deep breath, then nodded her head, yes.

We walked into the handsomely furnished room. Cards and flowers crowded the dresser top—from Life Center's welcome committee, since John had no family. On the bed lay a good-looking black-haired youth with a tracheal tube protruding from his throat. The tube was attached to respiratory equipment that wheezed and whined above the boy's head.

"Hello, John, I'm Pastor Blair from Calvary Temple. They tell me the news isn't good."

John waited until the respirator paused. "They said you might come today," he said. Another pause while the respirator whirred. "No, I guess I've had it."

For a while we talked about events we have no control over, about how difficult it is to believe we can find God in every situation. Then I prayed, placing my hand on his forehead, trying literally to be in touch with his hurt.

He blinked hard.

"See you, son." I said in a whisper.

"See you, Mr. Blair."

Although we had stopped selling bonds for Life Center we continued to sell securities for the various building programs at the church. It never occurred to me to question this. Why—

even if Calvary's cash balance went to zero (I smiled at the very thought), there were the buildings and property owned by the church. The Polo Grounds alone were worth three million dollars. This gave me a great sense of security, as I explained to a caller one day.

"Can you *personally* tell me that Calvary Temple bonds are safe?" she asked.

"Yes, m'am. That I can promise you. Calvary Temple is as solid as the First National Bank of Denver."

I remember saying the same thing to one of our salesmen. Howard McPherson was in correspondence with a widow who wanted to invest $21,000 with us. Howard wanted to double-check that such an investment was secure.

"Howard," I said, "you can rest assured. If we sold all our assets and paid off all our creditors, Calvary Temple would still be three million dollars to the good."

Crisis is not usually the result of one large overwhelming event. Oftener it is produced by a series of smaller aggravations. A seemingly endless run of anxieties and disappointments and frustrations.

It was just such a series that began accumulating at the end of 1972. First there were the reports from every quarter that the national economy was headed for a serious recession. Then there were the probes of other ministries, far more prominent than my own: Rex Humbard, Jerry Falwell.

More immediate breakdowns happened too. One snowy December morning our home telephone rang. It was Roy Hudgins, business manager at Calvary Temple. "Sorry to bother you so early, Pastor," Roy said. "But last night the furnace went off at the Castle and the pipes froze. There's been a lot of damage."

"Oh, brother!" I groaned. "And I suppose it'll take thousands of dollars to fix."

"You guessed it."

"Won't the insurance cover it?"

"Not everything. You ought to see the place. Somebody

really should be living in that house." The Castle had been vacant for several months; none of the staff members wanted the expense and responsibility of the big place.

An hour later, dressed in our warmest clothes against the subzero weather, Betty and I drove over to the Castle with Roy. As we tramped across the unplowed driveway things didn't look too bad: the brick-and-timber house with its hexagonal turret appeared impregnable.

Inside, however, the place was an ad for a horror movie. Upstairs we found the source of the trouble: bathroom plumbing had burst, cascading water ruinously through the house.

"We'll have to redo the whole place, of course," Roy was saying. "We could redecorate to your taste, if you're interested."

I looked at Betty. She stood with her hands in her pockets, breath billowing. "We appreciate the thought, Roy, but we really couldn't," she said. "It's just too overwhelming."

The two of them started back down the stairway. "Don't make up your minds right away," I heard Roy saying. "Let us do the basic work. Come back in the spring and take another look."

I lingered behind. I didn't need a second look to know that this preposterous mansion, with its beamed ceiling and leaded-glass windows, was the fulfillment of every daydream of a boy growing up in Enid, Oklahoma.

Crisis followed crisis.

We had a happy Christmas with our girls and their families. Judy and Roger had given us our first granddaughter, Kelly Lynn, born in August, 1970. Vicki and Jack now had a second little boy, Brian Charles, born in September, 1971. It was true, Christmas day both Betty and I picked up a subdued quality in Vicki, but we put it down to her pregnancy. She and Jack were expecting their third child in April. Then one morning in January, 1973, I returned from my daily jogging stint at a nearby school playground to find Betty in tears.

"What's happened, honey?"

"Charles . . ." Betty sat down heavily on the sofa. "Vicki phoned while you were out. She and Jack are separating."

The words didn't register.

"They're getting a divorce, Charles."

"But . . . Marrles . . . little Brian," I stammered. "And the new baby coming!"

Haltingly, Betty repeated all she could remember of the conversation. "But Jack's such a fine person!" I protested. "They seem so right for each other!"

For an hour we talked, saying the things you say at a time like this. But it was clear that they had already reached their own decision. Jack was going to start again elsewhere. Betty and I wept for his pain as well as Vicki's.

One morning at the office I had a call from our church accountant, Ralph Bartsch. "Charles, I need to see you. Right away."

When Ralph arrived, Joan Bjork and I exchanged startled glances. The usually nattily dressed accountant was disheveled, tie askew, vest only partially buttoned. He sat down on the striped, sectional sofa and spread out on the coffee table a set of notes. Figures were smudged, others crossed out. One sheet looked as if it had been wadded up, then smoothed. Joan went for coffee.

"Charles," said Ralph, waving his hand at the yellow sheets before him, "I told you a year ago I did not like the trend. But now. . . ."

Ralph showed me his arithmetic. Less than a year ago the cash reserves of Calvary Temple had totaled $575,320. During the past year, Ralph's preliminary figures showed, our positive cash position had been all but wiped out, largely through "temporary" transfers to Life Center. Calvary Temple was virtually insolvent.

We were both silent. Background noises became strangely loud: a car starting in the parking lot, a typewriter clacking away in the outer office.

"Charles," Ralph said at last, "why did you let the situation at Life Center get out of hand?"

The question, I knew, was the correct one. Even as Ralph was showing me the actual mechanics, how funds had been transferred incorrectly from the accounts of the church to the accounts of the Center, how imprudently large expenses had been incurred in the selling of Calvary Temple securities, even as he was going over the facts, I knew that the correct question was not how had someone made one mistake, someone else another, but *why did I allow it*?

I alone was responsible. As the captain of a ship is responsible for errors aboard, so was I for the business transactions at Calvary Temple and Life Center. My overcrowded schedule was a reason for my failure to supervise in sufficient detail.

It was not an excuse.

I met at once with the church's finance committee to let them know the details of Ralph's discovery. They took charge, selecting from among themselves an investigating team that included three CPA's. Within a week these men turned up the startling fact that there were perhaps 90 too many employees at Life Center, including some that appeared not to be doing much for their salaries.

In February, 1973, the State of Colorado joined the federal SEC in making inquiries about our financial affairs. We received a letter from the Colorado Securities Commissioner asking questions not only about Life Center and Calvary Temple, but about the Foundation as well.

On April 4, 1973, a year after our first letter from Mr. Krys, came the final definite denial of our second prospectus by the SEC. Garth Grissom called me at the office to tell me about it. "The SEC says further that they consider us insolvent."

I could think of nothing to say.

"Charles?"

"Yes, I'm here, Garth. I just can't seem to take it in. Does the finding include the church?"

"I'll send you a copy of the letter. It refers to Life Center and to the Foundation."

I thanked Garth and put the phone down. Overnight we were in a peck of troubles. Garth suggested that we call a moratorium on interest payments and go into voluntary receivership. But surely there was another way. What would happen to all the people who had lent us money? And what about Life Center residents like Jane Laybourn and John Folks?

And if we called a moratorium, the panic-edged thoughts continued, wouldn't this precipitate the very thing we had to avoid—hundreds of investors rushing to cash their time payment certificates all at once?

On April 11, 1973, I returned to Denver from a speaking trip to Dallas to be met at the airport with news that in my absence Wendell Nance had dissolved the Department of Development. He had called a meeting in which he resigned the leadership and dismissed the staff. It was clear to me that tensions even worse than those I knew about were getting to Wendell. This act, more than any letter from the SEC, told me the magnitude of the problems we faced at Life Center.

The monthly church board meeting was scheduled for April 24. At that time I knew that I, too, was going to have to ask the board to consider my resignation. It would be hard for me to step down as pastor of Calvary Temple after 26 years. But not only had I failed miserably to protect the church's finances, it was now clear to me that I could not continue trying to oversee the operation of Life Center from a distance. Someone had to focus on that project night and day. Who but me, now that I'd let it drift to near-disaster.

On April 24, 1973, nine days after Vicki's baby, Monica, was born, the 50-man board of Calvary Temple met in the Hearthstone Room at the church. For these men I reviewed our situation, how it was now definite that the SEC disapproved the prospectus for Towers Three and Four. How this left us with a quandary. Without selling bonds we could not complete the towers; without income from the towers we could not pay our debts.

I invited questions. Someone asked why we couldn't simply sell Life Center. We could, of course. But we had spent a great deal more for the facility than we could possibly realize at this stage, and we would still be responsible for debts incurred under our ownership.

Another possibility, I said, was to mount a mammoth gift-raising effort. I believed I was the person to coordinate such an effort, and to free myself to devote full time to it, I submitted to this board my resignation from all official capacities at Calvary Temple.

I had barely finished speaking when one of the board members stood up. I remembered that he had objected to the nursing home from the start. "Six-and-a-half years ago, as you all know, I went off this board because I did not agree with the church's involvement with Life Center."

He paused; 50 men fixed their eyes on him. "But tonight, I feel that we must see Life Center through, and also that Pastor Blair should stay in the pulpit where he belongs. That's your calling, Charles. You're a preacher, not a nursing-home administrator."

In the hubbub of approval generated by these words, a board member who was also on the finance committee was called out of the room. He came back in with a stricken face and a scrap of paper on which he had scribbled some notes. He handed me the paper. I studied it in silence: line of credit at the bank, used to the limit; other sources of ready cash, exhausted. I tapped a glass for attention.

"Gentlemen," I said, "here is the piece of news we all have been dreading. At the end of April—seven days away—Life Center will be unable to meet its month-end obligations."

With that, an amazing thing happened. Instead of being threatened by the news, the men around me seemed to feel challenged. One after another they committed their own money to bailing us out of this crisis. But the most important effect of the news was a shift in the spiritual climate of the meeting. Men stood up to say that we needed to support one another in prayer, on an ongoing basis. For starters, they decided on a weekly prayer time. Every Wednesday morning from six to seven we agreed to pray, each man in his own home, yet united in common purpose, girding one another for the battles ahead.

16

Wendell made his resignation official on May 14, 1973. He came into my office that afternoon and handed me two letters. He didn't even sit down, just laid them on my desk. Was it my imagination, or were there tears in his eyes?

I glanced quickly through the letters, one written on the familiar mauve stationery of Calvary Temple, the other on the white stationery of Life Center. "You say here, Wendell," I said, "that at times you made errors. But, Wendell, so did I. Since we both failed, don't you think we should try together to find solutions?"

Wendell didn't agree. He felt that it was better for the work, and for his family, if he stepped down now. I felt a tightening in my own throat: how different things would be at Life Center without this personal friend and his cheerful good nature.

We made an emergency appeal. From the board and from the church as a whole we raised $160,000 and paid our April bills. In May and June, the same thing: squeaking by with the end of the month looming like doomsday. I made one last effort at borrowing the sum we needed to complete the last two towers. This time the money would come from a bank, collateral to be property owned by Calvary Temple not previously used to secure bonds. On July 11, 1973, I recommended to the board of the church that Calvary Temple pledge assets worth $3,600,000 against a loan for that amount.

It seemed a logical enough step, and was approved by the board, so we made application. Although the *cash* position of the church continued as precarious as on the day Ralph Bartsch brought his crumpled worksheet to my office, the institution's underlying wealth, as represented by real estate holdings, remained, we believed, as solid as ever. The bank said it would try to have an answer for us in 60 days.

Sixty days! That meant nothing till mid-September.

Meantime, we had been trying to persuade Vicki to move. It didn't make sense for her to live alone with the new baby and two very active little boys. Perhaps she could move into a small cottage owned by the church. The cottage had originally been built as a pool house for the Castle. Betty could walk there from the church in three minutes beween Bible classes or choir sessions; I could join my grandsons for lunch.

So on a warm summer day, Vicki and Betty plus two husky fellows from the men's group drove a borrowed pickup to Vicki's house and came back to the former pool house with a truckload of belongings. The church's business manager used the moment to bring up once again the subject of our moving into the Castle.

"Someone really ought to be in that house," Roy said. "And the church could certainly use the rent you would pay."

It was the desire to be near Vicki more than anything else that persuaded Betty to put up for sale the home she loved on Happy Canyon Drive. Basic repair work had been done on the Castle after the water pipes burst, but the task of redecorating was huge. The tile used in the ruined bathrooms, for example, was no longer made. Replacing broken windows was equally difficult; each of the building's 88 leaded-glass casements had been custom made. Every bit of wood, every door had to be rubbed by hand to restore sheen ruined by water and dampness. Although most of the work was still to do we moved into the Castle in September, 1973.

That same month I received the report of the CPA we had hired to assess the financial worth of our three organizations. But . . . what figures were these! Life Center *$5.6 million* in the red? The Foundation *$1.5 million* in debt? Only the church, according to his findings, was in the black. And that by a mere $7,000!

I couldn't take it in. This independent CPA was saying that Calvary's net assets, after obligations, were not even worth $10,000, primarily because the church had lent hundreds of thousands of dollars to the Foundation and to Life Center. The CPA entered these loans as "without value" because of the financial condition of the two institutions.

On receipt of this report Garth Grissom recommended that we at once stop selling securities for Calvary Temple, as we had already done for the others. I couldn't believe it. Not the church too! Everything *looked* so successful—the jam-packed parking lot, the burgeoning youth program, our ongoing missionary work.

We informed the bank of the change in our asset picture and, understandably, they withdrew their consideration of the $3,600,000 loan. And thus, in October, 1973, Life Center once more ran out of money. This time, however, we had no reserves to fall back on. We could not meet the interest payments due to lenders, nor could we meet our payroll at the Center—the doctors, nurses, dieticians and maintenance men, the housekeeping and clerical staffs.

With our attorneys I drafted a letter which we mailed to the more than 1,700 people who had become investors in Life Center. We invited them to attend a Grievance Night meeting on Tuesday evening, November 6, 1973, at which time we would spell out the nature of the crisis we were facing.

That afternoon I closed the door to my office and tried to pray. But I could not loosen the knot in my stomach. I went home for a quick supper with Betty in the echoing unfinished kitchen of the Castle, then returned to the church. The fist in my stomach tightened as I walked down the corridor and out onto the platform.

The silence that met me as I stepped to the lectern was not the friendly quiet that often greeted me on a Sunday morning. There was an uneasiness in the overflow crowd, a brittle hostility that crackled in the air. As I looked out over the faces, I saw many parishioners but also hundreds of faces I did not recognize. Suddenly I felt very alone. Wendell was gone. Most of his administrative staff and all of the sales staff was gone.

"Lord," I found myself praying, "I know that I'm not really alone but what I ask for is the *sense* of Your presence."

As clearly as possible I described our position. The question period was angry. There were insinuations that investors' money had been stolen. Words like *extravagant waste* and *mismanagement of funds* were flung at me. It didn't make it easier realizing that we had not managed well, and that there had been extravagances. But *stealing*?

Toward the end of the evening I spotted some people furiously making notes at the back of the room. Reporters. Somehow it had not occurred to me that they would be present. At the close of the meeting I ducked through a side door and headed for my study.

I went through the dark outer office into the inner room. I left the doors open, but I did not turn on the lights. I sat at my desk in that dark room while people stuck their heads in the outer office, and went away.

"Oh dear God," I whispered, "here I am hiding like a criminal." Here in this room where I had prepared so many sermons on love and joy. Where I'd counseled so many people on solving their problems. Only when I was certain the church was empty did I emerge from the darkness and walk across the vast deserted parking lot to the brooding brick bulk of the Castle.

For a short while after that traumatic Grievance Night, things seemed to be getting better. For one thing, the new management firm we hired to run the Center instituted economies which, while not affecting patient care, whittled away at our enormous operating deficit. For another, we sold an option on the Polo Grounds. For yet a third, we were able to establish a new line of credit at the bank based on Calvary Temple's past good record in repaying debts. Our gift-soliciting program also began showing results. We raised a million dollars in pledges, plus enough cash to pay the delinquent interest obligations on our bonds.

But within weeks each of these hopes dissolved. The sale of the Polo Grounds ran into a snag. The million dollars pledged was generous but did not supply the cash we needed right now. Even the $150,000 line of credit we got from the bank was eaten up almost instantly, repaying anxious people who had lent us money, trying to meet even our trimmed-down payroll. With better management Life Center began to show a positive cash flow, but the $25,000 cleared each month just met the $25,000 monthly payment to Phoenix Mutual.

In March, 1974, we were once again unable to make our interest payments.

Word spread through the Denver financial community like ignited powder. Colorado Securities Commissioner Stanley Hays, who had been besieged by calls from our investors ever since Grievance Night, now took action.

"Charles?"

It was Garth Grissom on the line, calling me at home on March 13, 1974. "Charles, we've been served with a civil action by the Colorado Securities Commissioner's office."

He paused to let it sink in. "What does it mean?" I said at last.

"He wants the court to appoint a receiver, Charles, to take control of the corporations."

Garth recommended that we hire a specialist, Sanford Hertz. Next morning Mr. Hertz, Garth and I walked up the steps of the old-fashioned Denver District Courthouse.

Chief Denver District Judge Robert Kingsley met us courteously, and soon we were seated at a table in his courtroom while Judge Kingsley pondered a pile of documents before him. I noticed a man with a camera and a woman taking notes. The purpose of this meeting, Judge Kingsley explained, was to hear the complaint of Colorado Securities Commissioner Stanley Hays, who was seeking a temporary restraining order against further sales of securities by our three organizations, and who wanted a court-appointed receiver to take control of the corporations.

The State was represented by the assistant attorney general who, when Judge Kingsley gave him the floor, charged that our three organizations had engaged in "acts, practices, or sources of business which operate as fraud or deceit upon the public."

A white light seemed to explode in my head at the word *fraud*. As the shock passed, I realized that the light had come from the camera flash. The reporter's pencil flew.

There were detailed listings of our failure to disclose that our corporations were "sustaining substantial losses and were now, or would shortly be, in unsound financial condition."

Sanford Hertz and Garth pointed out that there were other factors to consider, that the church had an income of two million dollars a year and that I myself was hardly getting rich on my salary of $28,000. They said Life Center had 400 occupied beds and was at last beginning to show a return on investment.

The morning seemed to have no end to it. At last came the moment for Judge Kingsley's decision. All of us sat straighter.

Judge Kingsley agreed to let us, rather than the court, appoint three outside supervisors and an overseer who would try to come up with a program for paying off our obligations. He would give us and the Securities Commission time to work out a sensible plan. He hoped both parties would agree to this arrangement. We did so. Stanley Hays withdrew his request for a restraining order and his motion to place us in receivership.

I guess we were so hungry for good news that we found ourselves rejoicing as we left the courthouse, though in fact what had happened was not worth crowing about. We had agreed, in effect, that we were not capable of running our affairs and needed to be supervised.

"What about those reporters?" Betty worried, when I jubilantly reported the outcome of the hearing.

"Oh, I don't think there'll be much of a story," I said. "Judge Kingsley refused to issue the restraining order, you see. No, I think the worst is behind us."

The next morning my cheery mood persisted. Even the Securities Commission seemed to recognize that we were doing our best to protect investors, and that no one was going to run off to Mexico.

I took my grey suit from the closet and selected a grey-and-yellow tie to go with it. The sun was shining and there was the promise of spring in the air. I drove my car to the side door of the church, handy for a mid-morning appointment, then took a couple of minutes to stand in the sun-sprinkled sanctuary thanking God for all He had done for us.

During a meeting with my radio producer, and another with our men's choir director, my mind kept leaping to that 10 o'clock date with the architect. It would be awhile before we could launch another ambitious expansion program but we still needed to think ahead, it seemed to me, in view of the overflow crowds at every service.

The intercom buzzed: Joan reminded me that it was after ten already. I jumped into my car and was relieved to reach the Cherry Creek motel ahead of the architect.

There was a curious aloofness in the usually welcoming atmosphere of the familiar place. But I thrust it from my mind and sat sipping my coffee.

Until the man across from me unfolded his newspaper.

I fled from the motel, ducked into my car, and now, on a side street a block away, sat reading the newspaper account through eyes that blurred. I knew that I was parked on a street in Denver on an early spring morning in 1974. But in my mind I was seeing other streets, other years. The sidewalk in Enid, Oklahoma, where a boy waited with his milk pail. A trolley stop in Minneapolis. The flowers along Princes Street in Edinburgh.

I had heard that dying men saw their lives pass in an instant before their eyes. *Maybe I'm dying,* I thought hopefully.

And in a way it was death. For that morning, sitting in my ever-so-correct grey Oldsmobile, I took a look at myself. What I saw was a man whose entire life had been haunted by an ogre:

What will people think?

To be accepted, to be thought well of, had been the motive, I now saw, behind so much of my effort. Other people's approval mattered supremely; why else was I brooding here in my car on a little-used street? The fact was that I had made mistakes. But I had not committed fraud either in intent or—I trusted—in point of law. It was the *impression* created by a newspaper article that I was hiding from. It was my *image* that was hurt. And the creation and protection of that image, I saw with killing clarity, had been a major occupation of my life.

And yet . . . in the kaleidescope of memories crowding the front seat of that car, I saw something else. I saw a 17-year-old step into an unfinished building in Enid, Oklahoma and receive the unconditional love of God. That was real. That, and my love for Betty, had nothing to do with other people and their opinions.

Reality and image, I saw, were at war within me. I went over that thought again. Like every Christian I was accepted, *approved* by God Himself! It hadn't happened because I was popular or successful or wearing the proper tie—or because of anything to do with myself. It was the gift of God.

How was it possible for a Christian—who knew this Reality—to go on being concerned about appearances?

And now that I had asked the question, how could I break the pattern of 50 years?

17

Members of Calvary Temple were embarrassed, of course, by the newspaper story, but not as much as I expected. There was a decrease in church attendance, but a fairly slight one.

What hurt was when men in other parts of the country who had accepted invitations to speak at Calvary began to back off, all but saying outright that they didn't want their reputations tarnished by association with Charles Blair.

One old friend was an exception. On the Friday night before Memorial Day, 1974—how could I ever forget that date!—Willard Cantelon came to speak as scheduled.

"You've done a great job with this big old place," he complimented Betty, as we stepped into the sunken living room of the Castle.

The living room walls were freshly painted, the carpet was royal blue. There was a new sofa, upholstered in white and white drapes edged with blue to match the carpet. We had used some of the equity we had built up in our home on Happy Canyon Drive to do some of this. But now that it was done and we could entertain friends like Willard, I was glad we had.

"I especially like those flowers," Willard continued, and Betty's eyes glowed with pleasure. The custom-made bouquet of red, white, and blue silk flowers was the finishing touch to the nine-month-long refurbishing job.

Now it was late in the evening, after Willard's sermon. A group of us sat around my study at church, reviewing the inspiring service. One of the elders who lived northeast of town offered to drive Willard to the airport and I gratefully accepted. It was nearly eleven and I was ready for bed.

A fire engine went by on Cedar, sirens screaming.

Betty and I thanked Willard once again, then stood shaking hands as one by one the others left too. A second fire truck wailed through the night. It also seemed to be turning down Cedar. "With my luck," I told the last man to leave, "that will be *our* house burning down. . . ."

Betty and I closed the windows in the study. As we stepped outside into the chilly late-May night, still another truck clanged past on Cedar, dome-light flashing. Beyond, sky and trees were lighted with floodlights. On lawns along the street neighbors clustered, coats thrown over pajamas.

"Charles!" Betty cried. "It *is* our house!"

We began to run. Four huge ladder trucks were parked in our driveway: hoses crisscrossed the lawn while men with bullhorns shouted orders. How grateful we were that Mother Ruppert had gone to Patty's for the weekend! Searchlights played across the face of the house; black smoke boiled from an upstairs window.

In the group of onlookers in the side yard we caught sight of Vicki. We ran toward each other. "Mom! Dad!" Vicki kept saying, "I thought you were in there!"

Together we watched firemen break through the leaded-glass windows and play hoses into the rooms. Thanks to swift action, the blaze had been confined to a small area of the upstairs.

Spectators began to drift away. Vicki brought coats for us from the pool house. The trucks began to leave. From a neighbor's Betty phoned her mother and Patty before they heard the news on the radio. I called Judy and Roger and they insisted that we come over to their house to try to get some sleep. Vicki went back to her little house to check the sleeping children. Only an occasional fireman, now, wandered in and out of the main house.

"Do you want a light to get your valuables?" one of them asked Betty as we crossed the lawn to the garage.

"My valuables?" Betty glanced up at the black hulk of the Castle and I knew what she was thinking. Our valuables—what were they? The family was safe. We had the love of God and of one another. She had put months of work into renovation, but her valuables were not inside that house.

Firemen believed the blaze had started in the sewing room—perhaps an iron with a faulty cord. That room, they told us, was completely destroyed, as well as the large closet next to it. They had contained the fire in those two rooms but there was damage to the rest of the house from smoke and water.

Just how much damage, we discovered next morning when we came back, bleary-eyed, to see it in daylight. The electricity was off, which made the smoke-blackened house all the more dismal. Betty and I stepped onto the trampled mass that had been our blue carpet. There, sitting forlornly under the coffee table, where a sensitive fireman had placed them in an effort to keep them from water damage, were the red, white, and blue silk flowers. The drapes had been yanked down to allow the men to get to the windows.

About ten o'clock we were joined by a group from the church board, who accompanied us as we surveyed the disaster. The kitchen had a black line around the wall where six inches of water stood the night before. Everything in the house was streaked with soot.

"It's a good thing," one of the board members said, "that you have homeowner's insurance!"

"Yes," I said, "I'm glad the church takes care of that sort of thing."

The man blanched. "But . . . we didn't," he said. "Not for the Castle. You carried over the policy from your Happy Canyon house, didn't you?"

Which was the way we found out how bad the news really was. No, we had not continued the insurance from Happy Canyon on the contents of the house, the church and I each assuming the other was taking care of that. We didn't even have coverage for our stay at the Cherry Creek motel while the house was made liveable again.

The fire occurred on a Friday night. The following Tuesday, May 28, 1974, was the date our three supervisors were to present the results of their six-week study to the court. On Monday they informed us that they were going to recommend filing for Chapter 11.

"Do you understand what that means, Charles?" asked Garth Grissom, who was always careful to fill me in on the meaning of technical language. He was sitting on one of the twin beds in the little motel room. In simplest terms, he explained, Chapter 11 of the bankruptcy law protected a firm from being sued while it worked out its financial problems.

Valiantly, Garth stressed that Chapter 11 wasn't *really* bankruptcy. "It simply prevents individual creditors from bringing dozens of small suits, so that we can work out an equitable plan for the repayment of everyone."

Individual creditors . . . the accurate legal term, no doubt, but what I was seeing were the faces of men and women, some of them elderly, very few of them rich, who had believed me when I told them they could get their money back "any time you want it."

Judge Kingsley, too, was not soothed by the legal jargon. When informed by our supervisors—men we ourselves had chosen—that they had found the financial affairs of our three organizations in such a tangle that they had no choice but to recommend Chapter 11, he became "irate" . . . that was the term the newspapers used.

Far worse news, however, was to follow. On Thursday I

had a phone call from Sanford Hertz, the lawyer who had accompanied Garth and me to the hearing before Judge Kingsley. "Charles," he said, his voice betraying his regret, "you'd better expect a call from the district attorney."

"The district attorney? Dale Tooley? What on earth for!"

"Judge Kingsley is calling for an investigation of criminal activities."

The motel room with its cellophane-wrapped drinking glasses, seemed to spin around me. "Criminal? Did you say criminal, Sandy?"

"I'm afraid I did. Furthermore, I can't represent you because I work with the D.A.'s office."

I sank onto the side of the bed. "What—what happens next, Sandy?"

"Well, next I think you'll hear from Dale Tooley. Probably today sometime."

Sandy was right. Mr. Tooley called that afternoon to inform me of the judge's instructions to begin an investigation. What Judge Kingsley wanted to know was whether the money owing to investors had gone into our personal pockets.

My spirits soared. "I've got no secrets, Mr. Tooley." My mind went to the cardboard boxes full of old checks and receipts which we kept in an upstairs closet. "You're welcome to look over every check, every charge account, all my tax returns."

"Good," said the district attorney. "We'll begin the inquiry in a couple of weeks."

Suddenly it became crucially important to understand the sequence of court procedure in our country. Processes that had belonged to late-night TV were all at once, mystifyingly, part of my daily life.

"Well," Garth Grissom explained when I had shut the door to my office at church, "three things will occur.

"First, people from the district attorney's office will ask you a million questions. A D.A.'s investigation can take weeks.

"Second," Garth went on, "the D.A.'s office will prepare what is called a deposition—that is, a written summary of your case—which they present to a grand jury. A grand jury is a group of citizens called together for the specific purpose of deciding whether or not the evidence warrants a formal charge, an indictment.

"And third, if it should ever get to that, is a trial by a regular jury where the indicted individual is found guilty or innocent by his peers."

Just the words set my heart hammering in my throat. "But, if the grand jury fails to hand down an indictment there is no trial?"

"That's right."

And that, surely, was what would happen in this case. "Surely," I said to Betty, "the grand jury will recognize that although we committed errors we never lined our pockets."

Simply the fact of being under investigation by the D.A.'s office, however, I soon discovered, colored everything, including our ongoing troubles with our creditors. On Friday, June 7, I appeared before the U.S. District Court to argue against the appointment of a receiver to handle the church's receipts and disbursements. The courtroom was packed with spectators, many of whom I recognized. These were not the idly curious who follow any court proceeding, but people who had invested hard-earned money in one or more of the organizations I headed—Calvary Temple, Life Center, or the Charles Blair Foundation. Often it was my personal word which had encouraged them to entrust their savings to us.

Now I was being investigated for possible criminal liability. The fear-filled faces, the eyes which would not meet mine, told me more than any words of Garth's about the true impact of the D.A.'s involvement in the case.

Saturday, June 8. The newspapers carried stories about our effort to avoid receivership, showing photographs of anxious lenders leaning foward to catch every word of the hearing. Headlines, it seemed to me, played up the words *fraud* and *bankrupt*.

That same day, two weeks after the fire, Betty, Mother Rupert and I moved back to the Castle. It was far from ready: a fine ash covered table tops, books, dishes. Walls were coated with an oily film and an acrid smoke-smell hung in the air.

Once again workmen swarmed over the big house. At Betty's side, ladies from church spent days rubbing and scouring. A group went together to buy her a new sewing machine, and she set to work to salvage what she could of the water-damaged drapes and upholstery.

Every Sunday all summer long Calvary Temple was jammed, not only with our own people but with sightseers curious to get a look at the preacher suspected of criminal behavior. Some wandered up Cedar to stare at our house. The fire had drawn reporters' attention to the place where we lived; they made much of the fact that it was a "castle," while the working people who had loaned me their savings couldn't get their money back.

Again and again I went over in my mind the decisions which had led to our living here. Each one, at the time, had seemed reasonable, logical, even economical. But, for a Christian, is logic the only way to arrive at a decision? From the frozen water pipes to the fire, the place had been a gobbler of time, money and emotion. Was God once again trying to show me something? Had my reason for moving to the Castle really been Vicki and the needs of the church? Or was I still fighting a long-ago battle with the right and wrong side of the tracks in Enid, Oklahoma?

Where the Missouri joins the Mississippi, two distinct streams, different in color, density and temperature, flow side by side in the same channel for several miles. In our legal affairs, at first, there were also two independent streams. The civil action was heard in the federal bankruptcy court; the criminal charges were brought by the State of Colorado. The civil case involved our three corporations; the criminal case was against me personally and also against Wendell Nance, whom the D.A.'s office was investigating separately.

As Garth Grissom had foretold, Dale Tooley's staff spent many weeks gathering information. Because Sandy Hertz was unable to represent me in this case, I enlisted the services of an old friend, Arch Decker, an attorney and a senator in the Colorado state legislature. Most of the meetings with the D.A.'s staff took place in Arch's office. During one eight-hour session the questioning focused on what had become of all the money that passed through my office. Had I taken it to feather my own nest?

"We'll want to look at all your personal checks for the past five years," one of the investigators said. "I assume they are available?"

"Of course," I answered confidently. Betty and I kept our cancelled checks in a cardboard carton at the Castle.

"Good. Would you produce them for us, please? Tomorrow, if possible."

During the next break I phoned home, as always, to give Betty the latest report. ". . . and the D.A. will want to see our checks for the past five years. I wonder if you'd dig them out, hon."

"Oh no, Charles!"

"What's the matter?"

"That carton! Wasn't it in the closet off the sewing room? I'm almost certain that's where I put it!"

Then in the fire . . . I steadied myself against Arch's desk. I could hear myself explaining to a judge and jury that all means of tracing my personal expenditures had—inadvertently—burned to ashes. . . .

Betty promised to search every corner of the Castle and call me back. I put the receiver in its cradle, more disheartened than I had been since this whole affair began. Arch had ordered sandwiches sent up, but I could not eat. Nor could I keep my mind on the afternoon's line of questioning. Twenty years later, about four in the afternoon, the phone rang.

It was Betty. "Charles, those checks? After I hung up I seemed to remember two boxes, not just one. I looked everywhere and finally found that second carton. Charles, I almost didn't dare look at the dates. . . ."

Betty paused for breath while my heart stopped beating.

"The box that burned must have had ten-year-old checks in it. The recent ones, the ones we need—they're all here!"

During the long weeks of interrogation by the D.A.'s staff I saw very little of Wendell except to learn that he was going through much the same thing I was. And as time passed I began to feel hopeful. The hundreds of hours of questioning turned up not a single instance of money finding its way from a church program into our pockets. Investigators in fact expressed surprise at how little Betty and I had always lived on, with considerably less put aside for retirement than most couples at our stage of a career. The only investment we had was an apartment building in Greeley, Colorado, which had not required a large down payment and which we were able to finance out of its own cash flow.

So it was not the D.A.'s investigation, but the second of the two streams, the civil action, which at first worried us most. The federal court was talking receivership again. "Receivership would hurt," said Arch Decker. It was June 20, 1974. Arch, Sandy Hertz, Garth Grissom and I were having breakfast in a downtown coffee shop. "When the court appoints a receiver, it as much as says to the world: these people can't be trusted to pay their legitimate debts in a full and fair manner."

A receiver, he went on to explain, would have extraordinary powers. He would report to no board—in our case neither to the church elders nor the directors of Life Center. He could hire and fire at will. He would "receive" all money coming into the church or Center and parcel it out to creditors at his own discretion.

A quarter to nine. We paid the bill and walked around the corner to the massive new federal courthouse. In the plaza outside, TV cameramen and newspaper photographers were waiting, filming the four of us as we approached.

"How do you feel, Pastor? Are you going into receivership?"

The judge listened to the summation of testimony all morning and most of the afternoon. At four o'clock he handed down his decision. Both Calvary Temple and Life Center, he announced to the crowded courtroom, were placed in receivership; only the Foundation would be allowed to remain in our own control.

As the judge left the room, Garth spoke in my ear. "Our problem now," he said, "is credibility."

It was the middle of the night. I awoke completely, instantly alert.

Then I remembered.

We had a *receiver* at Calvary Temple. He had a name, too—Tom Hildt. He was a real person. He would own a house and a car and worry about inflation. And tomorrow this real-person stranger would be coming to Calvary Temple to take over the business life of the church.

Suddenly I wanted to flee. To get out of town! How could I continue to lead people spiritually when the courts held that I was not even capable of running our business affairs. Why not simply quit!

Agitated, I slipped on my robe and felt my way in the darkness to the library adjoining the big master bedroom. I closed the door but did not turn on the light. Summer moonlight streamed through the leaded-glass window. Perhaps I should just get in my car and go. Otherwise, within a few hours I would have to listen to this Mr. Hildt outline what Calvary Temple could and could not do with the money placed by faithful people in the offering plate.

I knelt on the brown shag rug and tried to pray, but God was a million miles away and there seemed to be a weight on my chest. The weight increased, closing off my breath, strangling me. I grabbed the leg of the desk, wondering if this was what it was like to die. Suddenly I was no longer acting at prayer.

"God help me!" I screamed, but no sound came from my lips. "Wake Betty up, Lord! Let her come here!"

In the bedroom next to the library, I heard stirring. I called again, soundlessly. Slowly, the door to the library opened.

"Charles?"

Betty knelt and put her arms around me. "What's wrong, Charles! Shall I call the doctor?"

I shook my head. "Just stay here. Don't leave me!"

For a long time we remained on the floor in the moonlight. In the peace which slowly settled over the room, I recognized that sensation of physical strangling as a symptom of my spiritual state. I *was* strangling in the thousand threads of our financial tangle. In trying to be accurate about a mortgage application in 1967, a phone conversation in 1969, I had lost sight of God's purpose working through everything that happens.

I needed desperately to get back to the insight that had come to me in the car on that side street, three months ago now. That morning I had seen myself through God's eyes—seen the pride, the posing, the hiding behind an image of success and acceptability—and seen that the pain was ultimately going somewhere. Seen that He could use mistakes themselves to change the person who had made them.

"Lord," I prayed as the sky paled with the first hint of dawn, "let me never again lose sight of the fact that You are in charge. You cannot do Your work in me unless I stay where you have put me. With Your help, Lord Jesus, *I'm not going to run away!*"

18

I knew from Joan's face that Tom Hildt had arrived in the outer office. "He's got an attorney with him," she said.

Mr. Hildt introduced himself and his lawyer, then in a crisp, civil manner got right to business. I sensed that he knew how difficult this meeting was for me: for my sake he was getting it over with as fast as possible. He handed me a letter that, he explained between puffs on his cigarette, spelled out the facts of his court-appointed authority.

"I think, Mr. Blair, that in the future you may wish to have your attorney with you whenever we meet formally." And then he added something which led me to believe that, although I was sure there would be times when his decisions would rankle, Tom Hildt himself was a sensitive individual.

"I have to see to it," he said, "that finances of this church are run in a businesslike way. But when it comes to the spiritual side of things, I will bend over backwards not to interfere."

And indeed, the most devastating blow to our dreams of so many years came not from the court-appointed receiver, Tom Hildt, but from the supervisors we ourselves had chosen.

They had reluctantly come to the conclusion that Life Center could no longer provide a home for our two neediest groups of residents, the severely handicapped and the retarded.

I had come to appreciate the importance of protecting our investors. But what would happen to people like John Folks, gallantly swapping jokes with the nurses to the pulse of his breathing machine? Or to the retardee who sold Amway products so bravely along the corridors?

It was all very well to say we would find comparable homes for them. It was fine to assure them that church members would continue to come visit them in their new locations. We did these things, of course. And yet the loss to us was immeasurable; I wept as one by one they departed from the white towers which were to have been their lifelong homes.

And meanwhile the two legal streams continued to flow side by side.

- The district attorney's office pursued its inquiry into possible criminal charges, preparing the deposition which they would present to the grand jury. I learned that five members of the D.A.'s staff were at work full time, investigating Wendell and me.
- On July 15, 1974, I began a second long session of appearances before the bankruptcy court, occupying the witness stand day after day for a total of 51 hours.
- The checks that Betty had found, undamaged by the fire, permitted the D.A.'s office to determine:

(a) if I had received any income which I had not declared to the IRS. (They found I had not.)

(b) if I had claimed expenses which were not legitimate. (Again, no.)

(c) whether the apartment in Betty's name in Greeley was a legitimate transaction. (They found it was.)

(d) whether we had made large purchases, at department stores for example, in cash. (They concluded we had not.)

As the criminal investigation continued to unveil nothing

improper in Betty's and my personal finances, I felt more and more encouraged. That only left my business life. Here I had made a lot of mistakes, but I was certain that the same kind of thorough investigation would uncover that these *were* mistakes and not an intent to defraud. I convinced myself that the grand jury, when it finally convened in December, would find no cause for indictment.

Still, proving my innocence legally would not change the fact that real harm had been done to individuals who had trusted their money to us. Day after day our mail brought us stories of hardships caused when someone could not get at funds I had promised would be available "any time."

I recall visiting one such couple, in a tiny unpainted house which reminded me of the ones I had grown up in. They had counted on the money they were supposed to be receiving in interest from Life Center bonds to make their mortgage payments. They wrote that they were now $700 behind and "we're afraid we'll be evicted."

November leaves blew across the lawn as Betty and I got out of the car. The man who answered my knock was probably in his mid-80s, a wisp of a person whose stoop made him shorter still.

"My name is Charles Blair," I said. "This is my wife, Betty."

He took an involuntary step backward and for a moment I thought he was going to close the door on us. It was clear from his letter that he and his wife had been following the case in the papers; what kind of charlatan he thought he was dealing with I can only guess.

"Come in," the old man said at last. We stepped through the door into an immaculate sitting room. The man's wife, as elderly as he, came in from the kitchen drying her hands on a dishtowel. When he introduced us, her smile disappeared.

We spent an hour with the couple, sitting awkwardly in overstuffed chairs with lace doilies on the arms, while I outlined the long-range plan we were working on to safeguard investors' money. But clearly, this couple's concern was not for the future, but for the mortgage due right now.

"And that's why we're here," Betty said. She reached into her purse and drew out a folded check which she handed to the man.

He opened it, then swiftly passed it to his wife. "Seven hundred dollars," she read aloud.

Our visit took a different turn now. The couple showed us through their home. We were introduced to the entire family by way of pictures in wooden frames. In the kitchen the lady took down a watercolor, painted by a great-grandchild, and handed it to Betty. "For you," she said. When it was time to leave they let us out the kitchen door. That, I think, was the highest compliment of all.

A month earlier, in October, we had sold the apartment in Greeley, our retirement "security." From this sale came money to help out hardship cases like that of the elderly couple. Also, in October, Betty and I had reached a personal financial decision: I went off salary, designating the money instead for the church's ongoing fund drive.

It meant, of course, that we had nothing to live on. But for years I had preached that God cares about the material needs of His children. Here was my chance to put my beliefs into practice. Was He our supply, or was He not?

Incredibly . . . no sooner was the decision about salary made than letters began to arrive unlike any we'd ever received. They came from friends in widely scattered parts of the country and each said in essence: "The Lord seems to be telling us that you have some personal need for this check. . . ."

These friends knew of course, about the crisis at Calvary Temple, and many had already responded to our fund appeals. But not one of them could possibly have known about our private decision, or any reason why they should specify that *this time* the money was "for you and Betty and the family". . . .

On November 22, 1974, a majority of our creditors approved the schedule worked out by Tom Hildt for repaying

$4.4 million in debt over the next several years. It was a major step and I was certain that in the time allowed we could raise the money.

Sandy Hertz was not so sure. "Everything hinges, Charles, on people continuing to have confidence in Calvary Temple. That comes down to confidence in you. You're the figure in the pulpit. You're the one they recognize on radio and TV. If the grand jury returns an indictment next month—how's a man standing criminal trial going to raise four million dollars?"

But—there wasn't going to be a trial! The grand jury wouldn't indict. It was unthinkable. Wasn't it?

So the two legal streams finally merged. Until the criminal charges were resolved, we would clearly be hampered in all our efforts in the bankruptcy case.

In late November Garth Grissom told me that he believed the D.A.'s office had completed its deposition and that Wendell and I would be called the following week to appear before the grand jury.

"That's going to be a strange time," Garth warned. "The grand jury room itself is a dark, dreary place in the City-and-County Building. You'll feel mighty alone. No spectators are allowed, not even Betty. You'll be asked a lot of questions that you've already answered a dozen times over and, strangely enough, you won't even have counsel. An attorney can be with you to monitor the hearing, but not to give advice. There won't be a judge, just a foreman.

"As for the composition of the jury," he added, "don't look for much sympathy. There won't be many professionals. Not many people who've handled large sums of money."

December 3. The day I both longed for and dreaded was here at last. Or rather, the evening was here, for the grand jury met at night.

Arch came by the Castle to pick me up that fateful evening. I said goodbye to Betty, wishing again that the strange rules of grand juries were different, and that she could be with me. Arch found a parking place in front of the City-and-County Building; together we walked down echoing halls to a door marked Grand Jury. Twenty men and women, including officers from our church who had been subpoenaed, sat on benches in the cavernous hallway waiting to be questioned. Almost the last person to arrive was Wendell Nance.

I saw Wendell so seldom nowadays that I continued to be shocked at the change in his appearance: thin, grey-haired, the bounce gone from his step.

"Hello, Wendel." I longed for a glimmer of the old Mr. Enthusiasm to enhearten us both. "I hope you're well?"

"They wouldn't even let our wives come," Wendell said.

My name was announced and Arch and I stepped into the gloomy high-ceilinged jury room. After the months of preparation the session had a strangely routine feel—almost as if we were walking through a formality. The D.A. stressed that the foreman and members of the grand jury were here to decide if there was a *possibility* that I was guilty. If so, then they should present an indictment.

Till now the D.A.'s staff had questioned me chiefly about possible irregularities in my personal finances. Tonight I was asked almost nothing about such matters. The questions instead focused on the sale of securities by Calvary Temple, Life Center and the Foundation, in the absence of prospectuses which spelled out in sufficient detail the risks to investors.

Abruptly, after what seemed a very short session, the hearing was over. All of us in the room were again warned that we were to discuss the proceedings with no one, not even family. I went to Dale Tooley and asked when we might expect the decision.

"Soon, Mr. Blair. Soon."

But it was two days before Arch Decker called to say that the grand jury could be expected to reach a decision that evening.

That night we asked Arch and his wife Lois, my secretary and her husband, Joan and Jerry Bjork, and a few other friends to join the family for what we hoped would be a celebration. Eight-thirty came. Nine o'clock. Nine-thirty. Betty served the "celebration" cake and coffee, and still there was no news.

At 10:00 p.m. the telephone rang. We all jumped, but no one moved to answer. The phone kept ringing. Finally Arch, who stood nearest the instrument, looked at me with raised eyebrows.

"Go ahead," I said.

Arch picked up the phone. Arch is a West-Pointer who still carries himself like a soldier. Now there was an all-but-imperceptible sag to the squared shoulders, and in that instant I knew I was going to stand trial.

"I see," said Arch. "Well, thank you for calling."

He put down the phone, avoiding the eyes turned to him from all over the room. "The vote nearly went our way." His voice was husky. "If one more person had voted for us instead of against us, no indictment would have been returned."

Beside me on the sofa, Vicki and Judy started to cry. Then everyone was talking or crying or asking questions all at once. I was glad for the bedlam because it saved me from speaking. At last, at a hint from Jerry Bjork, people started drifting out to the big circular foyer, picking up coats and scarves, making embarrassed goodbyes.

Arch lingered behind. "You have till tomorrow noon to report downtown."

"Downtown?"

"You know, to the—" Arch seemed to be having trouble getting out the word. "The jail. If you come in voluntarily, they don't issue a warrant for your arrest. It's a formality, Charles," he hastened on. "We'll have a bond posted before you even get there."

I scarcely heard. For the first time it was dawning on me that I was now an accused criminal, no different in the sight of the law from a man who snatched women's handbags. . . .

There was little sleep for Betty and me that night. As soon as I heard the paperman's car I was out to get the *News* from the box.

BLAIR, NANCE INDICTED:
PASTOR, FUNDRAISER ACCUSED OF FRAUD

The article reported that Wendell and I were charged with 21 counts each on the fraudulent sale of securities. Each count carried a maximum fine of $5,000—totaling a possible $105,000—and a possible prison term of one to three years in the Colorado State Penitentiary, for a conceivable total of 63 years. . . .

The possibility of a jail term was another thing that had never really registered. I heard Betty coming downstairs and hastily put the paper out of sight. "For the last time," I told her over a breakfast that we only pretended to eat, "I won't let you come . . . downtown."

I parked near the tall, windowless jail at the corner of 14th and Stout and climbed the marble steps. Surely the events of the past nine months were a dream and I was climbing these stairs, as often before, to call on an inmate who had asked for clergy. In the bleak waiting room sat Wendell Nance. It was obvious from the puffiness around his eyes that he had not slept much either.

At last an officer arrived: "We'll get you two fingerprinted upstairs, then go to the mug room."

As we stepped off the elevator a camera was thrust toward us and a flash lit the corridor. Black dots danced in front of my eyes as we stepped into the fingerprinting room. A huge full-blooded Indian stood behind the desk. He never changed expression, never smiled. He took my hand, put it into the ink, then said in a steady voice, "Twenty years ago I was driving my car listening to your radio show, Mr. Blair. I pulled over to the side of the road and surrendered my life to Jesus. I never dreamed I'd be taking the fingerprints of that same preacher."

In the "mug" room the police photographer was waiting. "Which one is Blair?" he asked. I raised my hand feebly.

"Wait'll my wife hears this! She watches you on TV."

In less than an hour it was over. I had become another of the thousands of men and women who each year are booked, fingerprinted, photographed by the police. Wendell and I were freed on personal recognizance bonds.

As I expected, the photograph of Wendell and me emerging from the elevator at the jail appeared in Saturday's paper with a follow-up story on the preacher indicted for fraud. How could I stand on the platform at church tomorrow? How would the congregation receive me after the news of my indictment? I got a hint of the answer Saturday afternoon when on my desk at church I found letters of resignation from two long-term members of the staff. Would I walk into church in the morning to find an empty building? I spent Saturday evening on my knees trying to gird myself for this possibility.

Our church services, being televised, had to start promptly. In the morning however, I delayed leaving the house till the last possible moment. I held the car door for Betty, then spent a long time backing out of the driveway.

We drove down Cedar . . . and both of us caught our breaths. The huge church parking lot was jammed to capacity, with cars parked on the street as far as we could see. Angry creditors, I wondered, my stomach churning, or just the morbidly curious, the kind who in the old days used to go to hangings?

I maneuvered into our reserved parking place and hurried Betty ahead of me through the side door. Joan was waiting for us.

"The sanctuary began filling up an hour and a half ago! There's not a seat in any of the overflow rooms. You'll have to hurry! It's two minutes to camera time."

Betty walked swiftly down the hall to take her place at the organ while I followed like a man going to his execution.

As I stepped through the door at the rear of the sanctuary, an unusual noise began. For all the world it sounded like clapping. The sound grew: it *was* clapping. Building, deafening, round after round of applause. Someone jumped to his feet.

Another followed. And then dozens and scores. Now the entire congregation was standing, clapping in unison, thousands strong, expressing their undiminished support for the ministry of Calvary Temple.

And all the while we whittled away at our gargantuan debt. The courts approved the sale of church-owned land along Cherry Creek, raising $1.5 million. A number of houses that could be dispensed with were put on the market, including the Castle.

Wendell's criminal trial, separate from my own, was at a standstill. Wendell was arguing that he needed a court-appointed attorney by reason of indigence. The judge did not agree. Claim and counter-claim consumed weeks and months of time.

That summer Betty and I found an attractive rental, a one-story ranch house in a pleasant neighborhood about a mile south of the church. After the Castle any place was bound to seem small, but with three bedrooms—one for Betty and me, one for Mother Ruppert, one for guests—the house on Gill Drive was certainly adequate. Mother and Betty set about making it home. The red, blue, and white silk flowers salvaged by firemen were given the place of honor on the table next to the sofa that no amount of dry-cleaning could make quite white again. Beside the flowers went Betty's Bible, the shadow of her bookmark indelibly imprinted in smoke on a page of the Psalms. Betty hung curtains at the windows, lining them with material from the ruined drapes of the Castle, put out pictures of the five grandchildren, planted a garden.

Only one cloud hung over the move. It happened on our first Sunday in the new house. We were leaving for church when we spotted an envelope beneath the front door. Betty reached down and picked it up. Inside was a note, hand-written in capital letters:

MOVE BACK WHERE YOU CAME FROM. WE DON'T WANT CRIMINALS IN OUR NEIGHBORHOOD.

In August, 1975, the court confirmed a schedule for the repayment of our debts at Calvary Temple. A receiver is appointed to manage the affairs of a financially troubled corporation only until it can come up with a Plan of Arrangement and the court is satisfied that the Plan will work. This meant that Tom Hildt would be moving out of the business office at Calvary Temple. A few moments after we received the letter officially releasing the church from receivership, Mr. Hildt came into my office, a smile on his face. He had obviously been planning for this moment, for in his hands he carried the few personal items he kept in the office.

"This is a great day for you, Mr. Blair. Congratulations! I honestly didn't think you'd be able to make it so quickly. Follow the Plan and I'm convinced you'll make it."

And with that our receiver walked out the door.

In some ways we could almost fool ourselves that things were back to normal. The church—though not yet Life Center—ran its own affairs again. With the church on a manageable budget, I went back on salary. For more than a year the Lord had continued to prompt friends around the country to send gifts earmarked "personal." With the resumption of a regular income—although, again, there was no discernible communication on the subject—this type of gift abruptly ceased.

Friends continued, however, to send donations, usually in small but always in welcome amounts, toward the horrendous expenses of the upcoming criminal trial. Even Wendell Nance's difficulties were going to cost us more than I could possibly pay out of salary, for I had to be present at his trial and represented by counsel. At first I had envied him the chance to have his case heard first and put behind him; now I was grateful for the opportunity to learn all I could about what I myself would be up against in a few months' time.

19

On November 10th, 1975, Wendell's case at last came to trial.

"Can you believe that it's been almost a year since the grand jury brought in the indictment?" I said to Betty as we drove through morning rush hour traffic to the City-and-County Building. We left the car in a lot and walked rapidly toward the massive grey-stone courthouse. Walking at a good pace when I was in public was a technique I had developed in the past year.

Arch Decker was waiting for Betty and me outside the courtroom door. The words "Criminal Court" were etched in the glass panel.

"Wendell still hasn't got an attorney," Arch said. "I think that's a mistake."

We walked in and got our first look at the room where, in short order, I, too, would be appearing for trial. Along the left wall was the jury box, a triple row of chairs behind a waist-high partition. On the far wall a window looked west, over the mountains. On the right-hand wall, upon a raised podium, was the judge's enclave: a massive desk, an American flag, and a leather swivel chair, placed higher than other seats in the room. The court recorder sat just below this desk; between him and the jury were the long tables where the opposing sides would sit.

Wendell sat at the defendant's table, now, thumbing through a stack of papers. Beside him sat his wife LaDonne and his three teenaged children, two sons and a daughter. Wendell looked up as I came through the gate. I took his hand.

"Hello, Wendell."

"Pastor."

I shook hands, too, with LaDonne and the children and said how sorry I was that it had come to this. Wendell looked over at Betty. "Tell Betty she musn't feel she has to come down every day."

Then the door to the hallway opened and in walked the dozen men and women, along with an alternate, who were going to decide whether or not Wendell Nance was guilty of fraud.

The bailiff asked everyone to stand: "This court is now in session, Judge George McNamara presiding." As he spoke a man in black robes walked in and sat in the leather chair. "Please be seated," said the bailiff. And with that the trial of Wendell Nance began.

Every day for the next two weeks I went down to the City-and-County Building, sometimes with Betty, sometimes with Judy or Vicki, sometimes alone. The basic position of the prosecution was that we had known we were in financial trouble at the time of various bond issues and had not so warned the investing public. As the testimony unfolded it began to look as if we had in fact made basic mistakes at Calvary Temple. The distinction I held on to was that of *intent.* If we had conspired to defraud, that was one thing. If we had simply made incorrect business decisions, that, it seemed to me, was another.

But even that hope was smashed when the prosecution dropped the charge of conspiracy. All it was trying to prove now was that in fact we *had* sold securities without a proper prospectus.

Wendell's witness to his Christian faith remained undaunted as ever. The *Post* and the *Rocky Mountain News* picked this up:

> One reason for the lethargic pace of the trial is that Nance is serving as his own counsel, assisted at the defendant's desk by his wife and three children.
>
> Nance described himself as having "no plans" for the conduct of the trial. "I have no idea what's to come . . . I really don't know what to do next," he said.
>
> Nance does not seem dismayed by the scope of his task. Facing counts of securities fraud, he says he believes the Lord will instruct him on how to carry one.

Here was a flash of the old Wendell. I could hear him now, in his office at Life Center: "If we don't get out on a limb, we'll never know what it's like to have God rescue us." His failure to obtain professional help, however, I felt was hurting him.

> Nance's lack of legal training was obvious. His objections were sparse and his cross-examination of the witnesses was really a repetition of the prosecution's questions.
>
> One veteran courtroom observer concluded, "by re-asking the questions, he's making certain the jury remembers every prosecution point."
>
> Nance ran into particularly severe problems Tuesday afternoon when he began presenting his own defense.
>
> As . . . Denver Deputy Dist. Atty. William Rapson objected to answer after answer, Nance at first looked puzzled.
>
> Then he would ask his witness to excuse him for a moment and explained, "I have to think over how to ask the question."

Finally, Nance gave up, telling his witness, "I was going to ask you lots of things, but I guess that will have to be it."

At another point newspapers reported that Wendell had requested 3,300 subpoenas for as many members of the church. Judge McNamara denied the request because, reported the *Denver Post*, "there wasn't time at mid-trial to issue such a large number of subpoenas. Nance explained that he just thought he should have all church members subpoenaed so that he could call those he needed as witnesses."

In another statement recorded by the *Post*, Wendell said that he was not responsible for the church's financial dealings, "because I didn't have the expertise to understand them."

> "I didn't know anything about securities," Nance said, standing close to the jury box and emphasizing his key points by writing them alternately with black, blue, and green felt-tipped pens on an easel.
>
> "All our sales materials were prepared by the corporate lawyers and our accounting firm . . . I had no background or frame of reference in this area."

Who then was responsible? I found myself asking. If Wendell Nance was not qualified, according to his own evaluation of himself, and therefore not accountable—who was?

Again and again I gave myself the same sickening answer: *I was responsible.*

I, and I alone. For if Wendell did not have the expertise to understand securities, as he said of himself, it was I who chose him, I who kept him in that sensitive position. I who did not supervise. I, ultimately, who let enthusiasm be confused with doing the will of God.

In ten days it was all over. Wendell made his summation. The prosecutors made theirs. The jury filed out.

Since no one knew when they would reach a decision, I was at home when the verdict was handed down. I heard about it, along with the rest of Denver, on television.

Wendell was found guilty, November 21, on 11 counts of fraudulent sale of securities. The cameras followed Wendell and his family as they came out of the courthouse, heads averted. My heart ached for them. I calculated the time it would take them to drive home, then telephoned to say how deeply sorry I was.

I could never get over the slow pace of the American legal system. Wendell Nance was found guilty in November, 1975. He was not sentenced until March 26, 1976. Although I had gone to court every day of his trial, I did not have the heart to go down to see him sentenced. From the papers I learned that Wendell had found two attorneys to represent him at the sentencing. The *Denver Post* reported Hal Haddon's plea in which he expressed the belief that Wendell's troubles came about not from evil intent but as the consequence of the very qualities I had loved in him:

> "You have to temper your faith in God with the realities of business," Mr. Haddon said. "It appears to me that the crime Mr. Nance is guilty of is one of far too much optimism without any tempering of business judgment."

Wendell was given a suspended sentence of 18 months in the Colorado State Reformatory. He was also fined $5,500 and placed on probation for five years.

Arch Decker now guessed that my own trial would begin in four or five months, perhaps mid-summer, 1976.

In the interim we needed to prove to the bankruptcy court that we could raise money to meet a Plan of Arrangement for Life Center. Without such a Plan we could simply be ordered to sell off buildings and equipment for whatever they would bring, and investors would be lucky to get 12¢ on the dollar. The Plan we proposed envisaged the return of almost all the investors' capital, and even some of the lost interest. The courts just didn't think we could do this. "You are under the cloud of a criminal indictment, Mr. Blair," said the federal judge. "Can you still raise money?"

So I set out to prove that I could. Once again, I was aware

that all my attention was focused on money. But—what other choice was there when we needed millions of dollars? I was constantly working to keep up excitement for these efforts. Some inner corrective voice kept nudging me: "Charles, haven't you learned something about *enthusiasm?*" But learning always seems to be a process, full of times when we slip backwards. And now as the pressures mounted, I fell back on the old patterns.

I auctioned keepsakes from my travels around the world. I raised money through energetic speeches. I organized rallies in neighboring states where the televised service from Calvary Temple was seen.

It was while I was on one such speaking trip in Minot, North Dakota, that I called home as I did each night, to find a fresh crisis waiting. Roger and Judy, now, were having trouble in their marriage. . . .

I spent the rest of the evening alternating between calls to the airline, trying to get an earlier flight out, and calls to Betty to say all over again the things we'd said half an hour before. When at last I got to Denver I met with Roger and Judy in my office for a long session of prayer and counseling. But as time passed Betty and I realized that the problems in the marriage—whether aggravated by my difficulties I never knew—were beyond our well-meaning intervention.

We were still reeling with Judy's news when another family loss occurred.

On Mother's Day, 1976, I preached, as I did every year, about my own mother. She was 80 that year. She and Dad still lived in Oklahoma, possessors, still, of few material riches and great riches of faith.

Betty and I had made the usual invitation again this year: "Why don't you plan to be here for Mother's Day?" The excuse this time had been a new one—Mother wasn't feeling well. "A stomach upset," she wrote.

The "upset," though, proved to be more than an excuse. A few days after Mother's Day Sunday, Dad telephoned to say that for the first time in her life Mother was in the hospital.

Betty and I caught the earliest plane we could; before I could leave the state I had to get permission from the court where my bail bond was posted. We flew to Ponca City, where the hospital was located. My brother, Bob, and his wife had arrived the day before from Washington state; Bertha Mae and her husband were there from Utah.

The exploratory operation took two-and-a-half hours and verified what the doctors feared: the cancer was inoperable. She had less than two weeks to live.

As soon as she regained consciousness and heard the news, Mother refused all further pain killers: "I want to be wide awake when Jesus comes for me."

To her delight she was allowed to go home almost immediately. And so a couple of days after the surgery we drove to Lamont, the little farming town in northern Oklahoma, where Mother and Dad had been living for several years. Dad and Bertha Mae rode in the ambulance; the rest of us followed in Dad's little Toyota. We pulled up to the dusty corner lot. I glanced at Betty. "No grass," she formed with her lips, smiling at our shared recollections.

There was, however, a large pecan tree in the yard. I remembered my visit here last summer. I had brought Marrles, who was six at the time. Marrles and his great-grandfather spent the afternoon rooting among the fallen leaves until they collected a basketful of pecans, which they took around to the neighbors. How like my father! He could never hold on even to the windfall of his own yard. For over 30 years he and Mother had served struggling churches in tiny communities, accepting no salary, staying only until a bona fide pastor could take over.

While Bertha Mae put Mother to bed I looked around the small living room with its sagging sofa and the gas stove which was the only heat in the house. "People have been so generous!" Dad marveled. And indeed every available surface was occupied by glass jars of vegetables and fruit and loaves of homemade bread.

Over the next two days we took turns visiting at Mother's bedside. Her own joy at her approaching "homecoming" was so contagious that it was impossible to be melancholy. Her only concern seemed to be the expense it might entail.

"Don't you dare buy me an expensive plot or a headstone," she said, shaking her finger at us all. "Just the cheapest piece of ground you can find and a plain pine box. I'm not going to be there in the ground—I'm going to be walking the golden streets."

Betty and I flew back to Denver for the services at Calvary Temple on Sunday. Tuesday I set out again for Lamont. The final leg of the trip was by small single-engine plane. In Wichita, however, a high wind kept light planes on the ground. I telephoned Lamont.

"Don't hurry, Charles," Bertha Mae said. "Mother died at four o'clock this morning." We were both silent a moment. "She went the way she wanted to go, Charles. She was singing a hymn."

The funeral was two days later. Bob, Bertha Mae and I shared the service in the little church. Mother had left this world with not much in the way of physical things. One very dog-eared Bible. A locket that had belonged to her grandmother. The little house in which she died.

"But what she did leave was immeasurably valuable," I said to the congregation. "The gift of faith that she bequeathed to us all, you here in Oklahoma, and her three children, each in full-time ministry."

With the center of his world displaced, Dad began to travel for the first time in his life, at 84 making his first trip to Denver. The first time he attended Calvary Temple the congregation gave him a standing ovation. Dad sat in the very front row and his booming "Amen!" could be heard all over the church. He was deaf and the "Amen!" sometimes came at odd places. When the service was over he could hardly get out of the building for the hundreds of people who wanted to shake his hand.

He visited Bertha Mae in Utah and Bob in Washington, and returned several times to see us in Denver. A year after Mother died he left Lamont for good and went to live with Bob and Lee and their four sons in Bellingham, Washington. His little home on the corner lot sold for $1,000.

20

July 22 was announced as the date jury selection would begin.

Friends from around the country were continuing to make designated gifts toward the cost of my defense. One friend of the church, John Dick, held a $500-per-plate Defense Fund Lawn Party. It occurred to me one day that I had never received a bill from Arch Decker. I brought this up with Arch one morning as he and I were going over the transcript of Wendell's trial one more time. "I don't think we ought to let that bill run too high without settling it."

"There isn't any bill, Charles. I'm donating my services."

I couldn't believe what I was hearing. Arch had a thriving law practice, I knew, but surely he couldn't afford to take off the weeks and months this case was taking! Arch was adamant, though. He wanted me to use the money instead to continue retaining the services of two lawyers who had formerly worked in the district attorney's office. "They know the ins and outs of criminal litigation. I don't."

During the last two weeks before the trial we met with these men, Jon Holm and Peter Willis, almost daily, rehearsing everything we knew about the history of our three corporations, the financial structure of the church, the trial of Wendell Nance. It was a time of mounting optimism, bolstered by the arrival of my old friend from Bible school days, Gene Martin.

On Friday, July 19, Arch Decker had a telephone call from the D.A.'s office. "I don't quite know how to interpret this," he reported to me, "but the district attorney is offering to plea bargain."

"To what?" I asked.

"To let you plead guilty to one or two of the charges, in return for the others being dropped." The penalty for a single infraction, he pointed out, would be far less than if I were found guilty of all 21.

I was silent. The appeal, of course, was immense: the savings in time, emotion and money would be incalculable.

I spent the rest of Friday and all day Saturday wrestling with the issue. I discussed it with Betty and our daughters, and with Gene Martin. I talked with my staff and members of the church board. Each time, all discussions came down to a single question.

Was I, in fact, guilty?

The more I had learned over the past months about what we had done in our frantic efforts to keep Life Center afloat, the more convinced I had become that we'd all fallen into the error described by Wendell's attorney: "Faith in God was not tempered by business judgment."

Each time a doubt was raised, I had pushed ahead "on faith." And in the process I became involved in a strange paradox. I had set out to build a nursing center to the glory of God. But the methods I used—slick brochures, high-pressure salesmanship, profit incentives—were the methods of the world. When they didn't work I simply applied more of them. I had pushed so hard, I could see now, because I believed we were serving God, and that He was therefore bound to rescue us.

I had not yet learned that all-important distinction between *faith* and *presumption*. We pressed the law of probability right to the limit, always expecting that just before midnight, at the 59th second of the 11th hour, we would be rescued. The prospectus would miraculously be approved. A millionaire friend would bail us out. The courts would waive the rules, in our case, and allow us to complete the unfinished towers whether we had money on hand to pay our bills or not.

None of this happened, and instead of being rescued we went under. The jury could reasonably find that members of our sales team (with me at its head) had failed to offer an up-to-date prospectus.

All of this was true. And yet . . . and yet we had not plotted to defraud. Intent—that, to me, was the issue. If insisting on this meant going to trial, then to trial I would go.

On Sunday morning I stood before the congregation at Calvary Temple:

"I must tell you of a recent development and of a decision. It has been suggested that I plead guilty to one or two charges and ask for the mercy of the court. I have prayed and I have thought and I have sought the counsel of praying friends—and I just cannot do it.

"So, it appears that the trial will start tomorrow. The events I will be asked to consider occurred between 1971 and 1973, and here it is 1976. Pray for me that I will be able to recall with accuracy, that I will tell the truth even when it hurts, and that I will act—and also react—in a way that will honor God."

Monday morning Arch Decker picked Betty and me up in his car. Jon Holm met the three of us at the rear of the City-and-County building. "I needn't tell you how important this jury selection is, today," Jon said, leading us up some narrow stone steps to a back door. "A jury can either work for us or against us."

On the third floor reporters waited. "How do you feel, Mr. Blair, having to go on trail for defrauding your elderly parishioners?"

Ahead was the room where Wendell had been tried. The bailiff ushered me, with the attorneys, through the swinging gate to the oblong conference table where Wendell had sat with his family. I moved aside the brown water thermos and white plastic cups and spread out my papers. Betty found a seat on the spectators' benches next to the girls and Gene Martin. We sat waiting. The floor fans barely moved the midsummer air. I looked out the window toward the mountains shimmering in a haze of smog.

The door to the judge's chambers opened and the bailiff summoned us to our feet. The judge in his block robes took his seat on the podium. "The court is now in session, Judge Clifton Flowers presiding. Please be seated." And so the case of the State of Colorado versus Charles E. Blair was opened.

Before starting the jury selection, the deputy district attorneys, Duncan Cameron and William Rapson, made it clear that jurors with strong church ties would be unacceptable. The logic was that churchgoers would stack the jury in our favor. Jon Holm got nowhere arguing that the opposite was also true: to select people with no church ties was to choose a jury which had in effect already made a negative decision.

Scores upon scores of men and women were called in. Most were elderly retired people, young people "between jobs," or members of "disadvantaged minorities." At last we had our jury—12 men and women and one alternate. They were a mixture of races and ages and backgrounds. Only one went to church regularly, a young lady who was a member of Judge Flowers' own congregation.

"What do you think?" I asked Pete Willis.

"Well," he said, "I just hope they have patience with complexities. Yours is not exactly an easy situation to follow."

Monday, August 2, 1976. The prosecution brought into the courtroom a bewildering array of graphs and charts and bank statements. These documents would establish, they said, that investments had been solicited by us without supplying an up-to-date prospectus. This, the prosecution reminded the jurors, was illegal. Further irregularities occurred when the Securities and Exchange Commission ordered us to stop selling the financial instruments and we had gone on doing so. They denied our claim that the SEC order referred only to Life Center, for which we had, in conformance with the ruling, stopped all sales, continuing only to sell bonds for the church and the Foundation. They would demonstrate that the three entities—Life Center, Calvary Temple and the Charles E. Blair Foundation—were really one. When the SEC ordered us to stop selling for one, we broke the law when we sold for another.

On this last point I felt fairly confident, primarily because the federal bankruptcy court was treating each corporation separately. If one court treated them as distinct, could another lump them together? But it was a complex distinction and as I sat there listening to the arguments and counter-arguments I remember Pete Willis's worry that such legal fine points would quickly lose the attention of all but the specialists.

The first witness to take the stand on Monday was our long time associate and in-house attorney, Warren Charles. Warren crossed the courtroom to the witness chair on its small platform against the west wall and was identified as the former counsel for Calvary Temple. He testified that as president of the three corporations I played an active role in board meetings. "He always sat at the head of the table."

Under questioning by the prosecutor Warren said that he became aware of our money troubles in the summer of 1971. It was true: I remembered Warren's coming to me with this concern. I remembered, too, the staff meetings in which I asked God to give us the courage to press ahead, "believing." Warren also acknowledged the memo he had sent to me in February, 1972, urging an updated prospectus with full disclosure of our mounting debtload.

"How did Mr. Blair reply?" the prosecutor asked.

Warren traced the crease in the knee of his trousers. "He said, 'You really know how to ruin a guy's vacation.' "

Other witnesses followed in rapid succession.

"What is your name, please? asked deputy district attorney Duncan Cameron.

"Pollyanna Cavett."

I knew Mrs. Cavett. She and her husband, a retired minister, had owned a house in Pine, Colorado, she said in answer to a question. While living there they had received brochures from Life Center, describing retirement apartments to be constructed there.

Mrs. Cavett testified that they had been offered a two-bedroom suite for $30,000, plus $210 a month in maintenance fees. In 1972, she continued, they had sold their house in Pine and put the money into Life Center. The move to the apartment, however, kept being put off by our representative, who said that the building was not yet completed. In June, 1973, the representative informed them that the apartment might never be finished, but said nothing about repaying their $30,000. When the D.A. asked Mrs. Cavett if she had been advised of our bad financial condition, she shook her head, expressing the hurt of everyone who had invested in our corporations.

"We just assumed," she said, "that everything was safe. We would never have invested our money otherwise."

So many witnesses were called that I found myself relying on the newspaper accounts each morning to keep the various testimonies straight.

The *Denver Post:*

> Investor after investor has said from the witness stand that he wasn't told of any financial problems.
>
> "We were given no financial reports," Mrs. Joseph Campbell of Denver testified Thursday. "We felt we could be serving the Lord if we invested our $25,000 in Life Center."
>
> . . . Mrs. Emma Jane Bickford, a widow, told the jury she had invested $45,000 in a trust fund on the promise that it would pay 9 percent interest. She had "no intention," she said, of making a gift to Life Center.

The *Rocky Mountain Journal:*

> The prosecution then called a long list of so-called "victim witnesses" who testified about their invest-

ments in the corporation.

Inez Caldwell, for example, testified she made two $50,000 investments in Life Center securities. ". . . I was told I could get my money at any time," Caldwell said.

Grace Barger, a shrewd, cautious investor, testified that in the spring of 1972, she began to get literature from Calvary Temple. A Mr. Brackett told her that Calvary Temple's assets exceeded its liabilities by some three million dollars. The woman said she was doubtful and called Blair on the phone. Blair, she said, confirmed everything the salesman had said and even went further. "He said Calvary Temple was as sound and solid as the First National Bank of Denver," the woman said.

On Thursday I was called to the witness stand. I sat in that wooden armchair with my back to the mountains a total of seven hours, that day and the next. Of the hundreds of prosecution questions, two stand out.

"As president of these three corporation did you know the details of what was going on?"

"No."

"Don't you think, as president, that you should have known?"

"Yes."

What more was there to say? I glanced at my family, sitting with the other spectators. As I caught Judy's eye she formed three words with her lips. They were,

"We love you."

The State rested its case on Friday afternoon, August 6. The following week it was our turn. Pete and Jon had already succeeded in getting four of the 21 counts dropped. Now together with Arch Decker, they presented the defense's side of the picture, portraying a group of people caught in an ever-worsening financial vortex, trying with each decision to protect money committed by previous decisions.

It was all very technical. I kept scanning the jury's faces for some hint as to how they were receiving it. As the floor fans droned on in the sultry room and the cross-examination went again over familiar data, several jurymen fell asleep.

At last the day for the summations arrived.

The State spoke first. Deputy District Attorney William Rapson asked the jury to consider one question over all: "Did the defendant know what he was doing, or did he have his head in a pillowcase?"

On our side, Arch Decker insisted that Life Center was a well-intentioned if over-ambitius effort to meet the physical, social and spiritual needs of Denver's elderly, and that if I had made mistakes it was through an excess of idealism. Pete Willis argued that the State's case was "prosecution by implication, innuendo and conjecture." The only crime they had established, in his view, was that of being "spread too thin," so that I had not been aware of everything being done in the three organizations.

Then it was the State's turn for rebuttal. My hands left smudges of sweat where they rested on the defendant's table. Mr. Cameron hammered home the point that we had failed to offer an authorized prospectus and had sold securities after the SEC told us to stop. His last statement was an analogy: If a man went to a bus stop and shot people—and then tried to help them get treatment—would that, he asked the jury, make the shooting less despicable?

The jury received its instructions from Judge Flowers and filed from the courtroom. It was too late, Jon Holm guessed, for them to reach a verdict today.

"Go home and get some sleep," Jon said. "Stay near a phone tomorrow. Someone will call you, and then you must come right down."

As my family and I stepped from the courtroom, the hallway exploded with light. A TV crewman, holding a portable camera and walking backwards, danced gingerly toward the elevator. Another man, holding a mike first toward his lips, then toward mine, asked the usual questions: How did I think the verdict would go? Was I apprehensive?

Betty and I held hands in the back seat as Gene drove us home. Nobody said much. We had done our best. Our attorneys had presented our story as accurately as possible. There was nothing to do but wait.

Friday morning I was awake early, but Gene, in the guest room on Gill Drive, was already up. We ate some cold cereal, standing at the kitchen counter.

At ten o'clock we knew the jury was starting to meet. Noon came. One o'clock. They'd be taking a lunch break.

I went over to my office at church. Arch phoned to say that there was no news.

Jon phoned: "I'm encouraged that it's taking this long. The longer a jury stays out, the better the chances for an acquittal."

I phoned home. "This thing could drag on for days, Betty. Why don't you go ahead with those errands?"

Vicki called. She wondered if there was enough time to take the kids shopping. I urged her to go about her business.

Garth Grissom called. A friend had offered us the use of a condominium in Vail. "You and Betty ought to get away for a few days, after the verdict."

"What if it goes against us?"

"All the more reason to take a few days off."

At 3:30 p.m. the crucial call came. It was Jon Holm. "The jury's reached a decision. Get down as fast as you can. I'll meet you at the courthouse."

I phoned home. Only Gene Martin was there. No time to try to locate Betty. Joan Bjork drove with Gene and me to the courthouse. Newsmen had long since discovered our back-door route and were waiting for us. "Are you prepared for the verdict to go either way, Mr. Blair?" The courtroom was almost empty, since no one had known when the jury would be back. I took my place at the defendant's table.

One by one the jurors marched across the room and took their seats.

Judge Flowers came in, hailed by the bailiff. He sat down. He asked the foreman if the jury had reached a verdict. The foreman stood up and smoothed his white hair. "We have."

"How do you find the defendant?" Judge Flowers asked.

"We find the defendant guilty on all 17 counts of the fraudulent and otherwise prohibited sale of securities."

The flush I had hated since childhood blazed up my neck. Deliberately I willed all expression from my face.

The jury had to be polled. One after another each juror was asked: does the verdict represent your vote? Yes. Yes. Yes.

It was excruciating. This cross section of people, the very ones we were in Denver to serve—the blacks, the Hispanics, the elderly, the unemployed—all giving their unamimous judgment on my ministry.

Yes. Yes. Yes.

The jury was dismissed. None of the 12 men and women looked at me as they walked from the room. Judge Flowers stood up and declared the trial concluded.

Judge and bailiff left the room, but I remained rooted to the spot. Behind me at the door to the courtroom I could hear Gene Martin and Joan Bjork parrying reporters' questions. I took four steps to the window. There, overlooking the city and the mountains, I wept.

21

Saturday the newspapers were full of the trial. The *Denver Post* had interviewed one of the jurors:

> Maybe the Rev. Charles E. Blair "should stick to preaching and stay out of the securities business," said Gerald H. Quick. Quick was one of the 12 jurors who found the pastor guilty Friday. . . . Quick said all 12 jurors were "positive we were making the right decision" in convicting Blair.
>
> In reflecting on the testimony about Blair's financial and religious empire, Quick said, "Maybe ambition got in the way of his (Blair's) common sense."

Ambition . . . was that at the root of it all? Had Gerald Quick put his finger on the nature of my malady?

My thoughts were interrupted by the banging of the screen door. Every Saturday seven-year-old Marrles and I had lunch together. Here he was now, prompt as ever. Vicki was close behind him. "He kept insisting, Dad. I told him I was sure you couldn't do it . . . today."

"Of course I can, Vicki. Today of all days." For two hours I wouldn't even think about juries and bond issues.

So my grandson and I kept our date. As always, Marrles chose the restaurant. This time it was der Wienerschnitzel. Marrles agreed enthusiastically when I suggested it would be "more fun" to use their take-out service than to go into the crowded dining room. We picked up our food at the drive-in window, then drove across the street to a deserted park.

"Aren't you hungry?" Marrles asked.

"Not especially, Marrles. Would you like my hamburger?"

"What's the matter, Grampa?"

"Sometimes, Marrles, the very thing you don't want to think about—that's the thing you can't get off your mind."

"Can I have your potato chips?"

Sunday, August 15, was my hardest day in the pulpit at Calvary Temple. It was worse than the day I had to tell our congregations that we were going into receivership. Worse even than the night I'd hidden from reporters in my unlighted study. Today I had to stand before my church as a man not only indicted for fraud, but found guilty.

"As you know," I began, "on Friday the jury found me guilty of fraudulent and other illegal practices." I confessed how confused I still felt about it: "I haven't put the pieces together yet." Betty and I were leaving for Vail after the third service, I said, to try in solitude to do just that.

There was no doubt, I went on, that investors had been hurt. And the hurt would continue. One of my chief worries now was that the conviction was going to make it harder to raise the millions we needed to pay them back.

And there were hurts that had nothing to do with money. Residents at Life Center had been hurt, as had all who looked to the church for leadership. "Every one of you in this room has had the devastating experience of opening your newspaper to read that your senior pastor has been found guilty of fraud. But that's one thing about which I am not confused. I am not this church. You are. One Christian can fall, or two, or three. But the church is Christ's own Body—and He can never be defeated."

We had parked our car, packed and ready, close to the side entrance. Now, while the last congregation was singing the parting hymn, Betty and I slipped out.

As we drove out of town our numbness was so profound that neither of us could find anything to say. I don't believe we spoke more than a dozen words until we reached Idaho Springs, 40 miles from Denver. I rolled down the window and breathed deep of the cool mountain air.

"Do you want to eat?"

"Yes, let's, Charles."

In the restaurant we bowed our heads to ask the blessing. Neither of us, though, would trust his voice to pray aloud, we were that close to tears.

Gradually, as we ate, the words came. Betty told me about a woman who had come to the house on Gill Drive a few days ago, gathering information for the Denver directory.

"She asked our name," Betty said, laying down her fork. "And you know what I did? I started to cry, Charles. I couldn't help it. I stood there on our front steps and cried because I had to give someone our name."

So then I told Betty about Saturday's lunch with Marrles, when I didn't want to get out of the car and go into der Wienerschnitzel. It was good for us to get these things out.

One subject, however, neither of us would speak about: the unknown sentence hanging over my head. Pete Willis guessed it would be four months before we knew what kind of punishment Judge Flowers would impose. In spite of myself my mind kept doing the arithmetic. With up to three years in prison and a $5,000 fine on each of the 17 counts—that added up to $85,000 and 51 years in jail. With Watergate still reverberating through the land, judges were being harder on "white collar" crime, and it seemed to me entirely possible that I might go to jail. I thought about these things, as we finished our lunch, but I did not say them aloud.

In Vail we located the condominium Garth had borrowed

for us. We unpacked, then I set off on foot into the hills to find a place where I could seek the Lord alone. About two miles outside town I found an abandoned cabin deep in a forest of "quakies," as Coloradans call aspen trees. The foliage, that high in the mountains, was already beginning to turn.

For two weeks I left the condominium at five o'clock each morning and tramped through the chilly mountain dawn to my hideaway. I stayed in that aspen grove until midday. I prayed. I read the Bible. I asked the Lord to continue His corrective work in me, no matter what the pain.

One morning He told me: *You should have been doing this all along. Come apart! It is difficult,* the Lord whispered into my mind, *to talk to you on the run.*

But now that He had my attention, there were many things He wanted to say. He told me that when we are over-concerned with image, it is because we feel our true self is somehow not good enough. He showed me that boy growing up in Enid, ashamed of who and what he was. He showed me that though my commitment to Him had never wavered since the night when Sister Buffum and I walked to the altar rail, part of me was still that boy, longing for the acceptance of others because I had not accepted myself.

He talked to me, too, about the dreams He plants within us. My love for the elderly, he seemed to say, came straight from Him. "But son, there is more to My call than a shining vision."

There were three ingredients to each God-given dream, He told me. The *method* and the *timing* were as important as the *goal.*

"And here is where you stopped listening, Charles. You caught My vision and then galloped ahead without learning how I wished to bring it about." The speed which seemed so crucial to me, the bigness which I equated with "doing things for God"—these, I began to see, were my additions to a perfect plan that I never stopped to discover.

Above all, during those mornings in the aspen grove, He told me that He loved me. "You've made mistakes—that's human nature. I've forgiven you—that's My nature."

In His eyes, He said, I was of infinite value. No achievement of mine could add to that value. No failure could diminish it. The price for my sin had been paid in full on Jesus' cross. The slate was clean.

As the days of solitude and the nights of communion with Betty did their healing work, I felt the burden of guilt and shame lift from my soul. I returned to Denver 18 pounds lighter and wearing a two-week-old beard.

And promptly forgot the word I had heard on the mountaintop.

The beard proved strangely symbolic. I came back from Vail knowing that tough times lay ahead: the sentencing, the struggle to raise millions of dollars hampered by the stigma of a felony conviction. And yet, I came back with a strange new confidence. It was based on the bedrock fact of God's love for me, rather than the self-generated, revved-up confidence we'd relied on before.

But whatever the source of my peace, it was resented.

Creditors, newsmen, even friends, did not want me to be joyful. Even my beard was attacked. I was condemned and I should be suffering. The word "callous" appeared in a newspaper piece; I had hurt others and here I was bearded, tanned, relaxed.

And I, who had glimpsed God's reality, fell once more into the trap of considering how I appeared to other people. Better be careful not to give offense. . . . Gradually I laid aside the freedom God had given me, just as I packed my hiking socks away in mothballs. Along with my responsibilities, I picked up the crushing sense of guilt. A week after we returned from Vail I shaved off my beard.

December 17, 1976. The trial had ended almost four months ago, during muggy August weather. Now the temperature had turned Colorado-cold. Christmas carols came over the radio; cars sprouted roof racks and skis.

Today I was to be sentenced.

There was no way of knowing how the session would go. "You have to take into account the mood of the day," Arch said as he and Betty and I drove toward the courthouse. "After Watergate, public accountability is the big issue."

"But," I said, "don't you think we're being the most accountable if I stay on the job and keep paying off those debts?"

"That's how we're pleading."

On the third floor of the City-and-County Building television cameramen and reporters were poised with the usual floodlights and questions. One last time we walked through the door to the crowded courtroom overlooking the snow-covered mountains. I nodded to the now-familiar bailiff and felt a rush of gratitude as I saw how many friends from church had come to be with us. They almost filled the spectators' section; in the front row Judy and Vicki had saved a seat for Betty. I pushed open the swinging gate and for the last time sat down with my attorneys at the defendant's table.

One last time the bailiff called us to order as Judge Flowers swept in, robes rippling, and took his seat above the rest of us.

The afternoon-long hearing began. The prosecution stressed the need for a jail sentence. "Public example" was the argument. The public should know that it had rights, and when these rights were trampled upon, they would be defended. We argued that it was in the public's best interest to keep me at the church working to raise money against our indebtedness.

At last the moment came for Judge Flowers to announce his decision.

His conclusion, he said, was that I should . . . I caught Betty's eye and held it . . . that I should be fined $12,750 and be placed on five years' probation.

People were rushing to Betty, hugging her. Others tried to come through the swinging gate and were stopped by the bailiff. Judge Flowers rapped for order. He had something further to say. He wanted it understood that the fact that I was a clergyman had in no way affected his handling of my case;

he had treated me neither more leniently nor more harshly than he would any other citizen.

He ordered me to report once a month to my probation officer. "I want regular reports on the repayment efforts and copies of the bankruptcy-court Plans for returning the funds to investors.

"I am satisfied," he said, summing up his decision, "that the only way the creditors can hope to be repaid is if Blair remains at the helm of Calvary Temple. My major concern is for the investors."

The gavel went down. The trial was over. At last Betty was permitted through the gate and we clung together.

Christmas Eve, 1976, I reported for the first time to my probation officer. Probation headquarters are located in the old courthouse, just a few streets from our original church building at 4th and Grant. Urban renewal has torn down most of the surrounding blocks so that the old court stands alone now. *The way I feel*, I thought, as I made my slow trek up the flight of stone steps, suddenly sorry that I had asked Betty not to come.

In the entrance hall a series of homemade posters carried thought-provoking messages. "Drugs are a drag," and "Stealing—is it worth it?" The waiting room was crowded with men and women, each facing his own ongoing confrontation with the law. I was the only man wearing a suit. I took my place on the pew-like benches lining the walls.

At last my name was called. My probation officer was a red-haired young man half my age. His first few questions were the standard ones put to any felon:

"Have you been carrying firearms?"

"Are you on drugs?"

"Have you opened any new checking accounts?"

Then they became more focused. The officer wanted to know the status of our repayment program. I told him that in a few months we hoped to have final approval from the federal court for Life Center's Plan of Arrangement. I added that we were ahead of schedule on the church's Plan.

And the first of these visits that were to be the monthly punctuation marks of my life was behind me.

In February, 1977, Wendell once again came before the court. To my great gratitude, ten of the eleven felony charges against him were dropped. The charges were dismissed because the assistant attorney general agreed that there had been errors in the presentation of Wendell's case to the jury. The *Denver Post* carried the story:

> Rapson pointed out that the D.A.'s office was anxious to convict Nance on a felony. The one remaining count will achieve that purpose. Nance agreed to the plea arrangement because he is "trying to rebuild his life."

On March 9 the bankruptcy court approved the Plan of Arrangement for the Charles E. Blair Foundation; on July 8 it approved the Plan for Life Center. In graduated steps over an 11-year time span, we proposed to pay back ten million dollars to Life Center investors.

Over the next three years we made major strides toward the repayment of our obligations. At the time I write it is early 1981. Although occasionally we may have to be late in making a payment, here is the basic situation:

- *Calvary Temple:* The five year Plan has been completed ahead of schedule. We finished paying off our principal indebtedness in September, 1980.
- *The Foundation:* We are current. Foundation investors will get back the principal agreed upon by the Plan.
- *Life Center:* Here, of course, we had the largest debt to repay. And here, ironically, we are having cash flow problems with the State of Colorado, the same state which brought us to court for not paying our debts. Colorado has been consistently late in its own payments to us for contracted services

(care of the elderly who qualify for state support), sometimes as much as $100,000 at a time. We are not alone in the problem. Many health facilities are closing down altogether because of similar slow reimbursement by the government.

Our investors' interest here, then, can be served in one of three ways. We can close the Center to keep from going further into debt. We can continue with massive fund-raising efforts. Or we can sell the facility to a qualified nursing home operator.

As I write in February, 1981, this last option seems the best route to follow. Our investors are going to vote next month on whether to accept an offer for the purchase of Life Center. Including the money already repaid to them, such a sale ought to recoup for investors a little over half of their original principal.

Doing our best with our debts, however, was only part of the job. A deeper kind of restoration was also needed. In spite of the church's support of Betty and me, I knew that my actions had caused bitterness to many, and that somehow I must try to heal this.

It was Arch Decker who suggested the Forgiveness Desserts, evenings when groups from church and community could bring their feelings out in the open.

We did just that, inviting anyone who cared to, to join us at 20 separate dessert-and-coffees. I fasted and prayed for 24 hours before each of these meetings. As few as 30, as many as 400 people showed up. I opened each by stating that I could understand bitterness toward me. This was everyone's chance to ask questions.

"We have to quit playing church," I said, "and be honest with each other."

And honest we were. People brought out anything from financial loss to the embarrassment this situation had caused them before non-believing friends and family. I talked about my own hurt. After airing our feelings we asked each other for forgiveness.

It was an exhausting time, and certainly not all the emotional damage was undone. Nonetheless the Desserts achieved a deep healing within the church and beyond. People who had drifted away started attending Calvary Temple again. As word spread through Denver that we were working on the subject of forgiveness, a surprising fallout occurred. Everyone, it seemed, had lingering resentment somewhere in his life; people were able to bring up things that had nothing to do with the situation at Calvary Temple. The relief people felt, the joy that came as a result of these forgiveness sessions were, I think, responsible for our being able to take a final step in the process of making amends: *protection against a repeat of the same mistakes.*

Prayerfully we set up a system of checks-and-balances in the business life of the church. Expenditures of more than $5,000 must have the approval of the board. No church program can pay out more than it takes in. I am submitted to the board and the elders in a brand-new way. As a result I am also freer than I have been in 30 years to spend myself in prayer and listening, preparing the church for the challenges of the 80s.

But this is only part of the protection we had to have. I also needed to submit myself to a small group, meeting weekly for support and correction on a personal level. In Calvary Temple today we have scores of small Agape Groups, made up of men and women led by the Spirit of God, trained, eager and able to live into one another's lives.

Along with the rest of the church, Betty and I are members of an Agape Group. It has not been easy to fracture the image of "pastor" and become just another groping Christian—though the debacle of the past few years has helped! I feel confident that if ever in the future I should begin to take a course of action which members of our group felt was wrong, not one of them would let it go unchallenged.

So, making *reparation*, seeking *healing*, defending ourselves from a *repetition*—these were the classic three steps that anyone must take to repair a wrong, and we were working at them all. Why then was my heart so heavy? Why, doing everything I knew to set things straight, did I still feel crushed under the weight of my failures?

It was my old, dear friend Gene Martin who brought me full circle.

He was back in Denver on one of his periodic visits. Judy and Vicki had joined Betty, Mother, Gene and me for dinner on Gill Drive. I was struggling with the blues again that night.

"I'll never be out from under this thing!" I exploded. "I'll never be rid of the debt—or the guilt."

To my astonishment, Gene laughed aloud. "Of course you won't, Charles! Haven't you yet learned the secret?"

"Secret?"

"The Christian's secret—when he makes a mistake."

The table was unusually still. Mother Ruppert leaned forward, wondering perhaps what her share was in the tragedy of Virgil Ruppert's life. Vicki and Judy had spoken frankly that evening of the errors they had made in their own marriages. All of us needed to learn how to live with mistakes. What was this Christian secret?

"The secret," Gene said, "is to realize that you never *are* going to be free of some debt, somewhere. You never *are* going to be free from blame. As human beings we don't simply feel guilty, we *are* guilty. As long as we're on this earth, we're going to go on making mistakes. We're going to go on sinning.

"And, correctly, each time we'll do what we can to undo the damage.

"Meanwhile, however, we feel defeated by our sin. And *this* is what the Lord came to change. You found the secret at Vail, Charles. I saw it in your eyes when you and Betty came back. You were a lot deeper in debt then than you are now. For all you knew, you were going to jail. Yet until you began to apply the world's standards to the situation, you were a free man.

"Go back to that freedom, Charles! Accept the love you were given at Vail. Of course you have to make amends for were given at Vail. Of course you have to make amends for your mistakes. All of us do. But in the very process itself—while things are still chaotic and wrong and full of pain—we can live as the forgiven, beloved children of God."

I can report that this is a truth which is becoming real. As spring, 1981, approaches, we have a thriving, Christ-centered church with its primary emphasis on giving to others. We are making steady progress in the repayment of our debts. We live in an atmosphere of freedom from guilt, even though guilty. We live in an atmosphere of freedom from debt, even though debtors. It is the special, treasured inheritance of the Christian that he does not have to be infallible. He only has to know the love of the infallible God.

Tomorrow we're going to Vail again. It is a ritual with Betty and me to get up into the mountains as often as we can. We go for renewal and rejoicing and drawing close to the Lord.

We go to reconfirm to ourselves this heritage which is ours—the heritage of unconditional love.

Charles Blair has donated all royalties from the sale of this book to Calvary Temple for the purpose of reducing debt.

Lessons in Listening

I don't believe that God has us go through either success or failure for ourselves alone. My experience happened to come through attempting to build a geriatric center, but the things I learned could apply equally well to anyone in the act of building: a young couple building a home, a career woman getting started, the officer of an organization. All of us are in the process of creating. All of us can face some variation of the temptations which beckoned me.

And so I've spent time reviewing what happened at Calvary Temple. The process of transformation is still going on. I have not achieved complete, permanent release from old habit patterns, but I have some hearing aids I didn't have before:

Test the spirit behind your dreams.

The Bible tells us to try spirits to see if they are of God (First John 4:1). To this day I am confused as to whether that original vision for Life Center came from God or from my own ego. Seen as guidance, it appeared to have lots of confirmation. But there were persistent Christian voices challenging this.

Unity between husband and wife.

The primary person to question my dream was Betty. She objected with gentleness, because this is her nature. But I never doubted her position. We were not in accord. Today I would not dare violate the injunction of Ephesians 5:21, that we be submitted one to another. I never *really* prayed through this major project with Betty until we were of one heart and one mind. I never *really* submitted my dream until we reached the place where we could say, "It seemed good to the Holy Spirit and to us" (Acts 15:28) to proceed.

Seek a Body of spiritual peers.

The protection a husband and wife provide each other can be extended (or supplied, for the unmarried) by entering into relationship with a small group of men and women committed to lift one another regularly to the Throne of Grace. Such a group provides not only support but—crucial in any time of building—correction. This is what makes spiritual peerage: not age or education or social position, but the willingness to speak the truth in Christ.

Are your co-workers a completion of yourself?

Or simply an extension? Ideally, in any Christian undertaking, there will be as many facets of Christ's personality represented as possible. If I am called to leadership and find helpers who are simply echoes of myself, I double my strengths but I also double my weaknesses.

I spent too much time reasoning, not enough in storming heaven.

When time is short, the most important way we can use it is in prayer. In any crisis there comes a time when human logic is worthless. Then we need the tools which are available to us as children of God. More-than-usual *doing* must be balanced with more-than-usual *praying*.

Impatience was my biggest problem.

I simply couldn't wait. Today I have committed myself to a new route: when *my* timing is thwarted I will divert my restlessness to prayer and *do nothing* until I have a clear directive from God, confirmed by the Body. Then we will put our feet where He has trod.

Catching God's vision is only half the battle.

The second half is discovering His means for bringing it about. We know His objectives by revelation. The battle plan will have to come by revelation too. It will probably be different from any plan we could have devised. What human being, after all, would have thought of blowing trumpets before a walled city!

Beware of prior successes.

The success of yesterday tempts us to lean on a formula rather than on God. Moses struck the rock with his staff and water gushed forth. When he tried to provide water the same way a second time, God reproved him. Faith is progressive. At Calvary Temple we mixed fund raising with borrowing, successfully. At Life Center we repeated this mix—to our sorrow. We weren't allowing God to take us another step in discipleship.

Faith versus presumption.

When we faced obstacles I kept telling myself that no great endeavor is without opposition. I'd "believe" my way through every difficulty. I made the mistake of having faith in faith. What God calls us to, however, is faith in Him—and Him alone. I have to be certain that I am believing in God, and not in my own willpower.

To sum up: there are three things to listen for: **The Dream. The Method. The Timing.**

We must hear His voice on all three. And that can occur only through much listening. We did this naturally as we were building Calvary Temple. But by the time Life Center came along we were pretty successful, and certainly we were busy. We just did not take the scores, the hundreds of hours necessary to ask:

Is the dream *His* vision?
Is the method *His* way?
Is the timing *His* moment?